Secret Realities of Hajj

By
Mawlana Shaykh As-Sayed Nurjan Mirahmadi

PUBLISHED BY THE

NAQSHBANDI CENTER OF VANCOUVER

Secret Realities of Hajj Copyright © 2017 by
Mawlana Shaykh As-Sayed Nurjan Mirahmadi

ISBN: 978-0-9958709-0-1

All rights reserved.

No part of this book may be used or
reproduced in any manner whatsoever
without written permission.

Published and Distributed by:

Naqshbandi Center of Vancouver

3660 East Hastings

Vancouver, BC V5K 4Z7 Canada

Tel: (604) 558-4455

Web: nurmuhammad.com

First Edition: January 2017

TABLE OF CONTENTS

ABOUT THE AUTHOR i
UNIVERSALLY RECOGNIZED SYMBOLS vii
HAJJ IS 'ARAFAT 1
REALITY OF HAJJ 15
REALITY OF TAWAF (CIRCUMAMBULATION) 27
THE SECRETS OF THE 12TH MONTH OF THE ISLAMIC LUNAR CALENDAR DHUL HIJJA ذَالْحِجَّة 41
REALITIES OF THE CIRCLE AND SECRETS OF HAJJ 55
REALITY OF HAJJ 63
THE SEVEN SPRINGS OF REALITY 81

Appendix 1 97
   Welcoming the Holy Month of Dhul Hijjah and 'Arafah

Appendix 2 99
   Fasting in the First Ten Days of Dhul Hijjah

Appendix 3 101
   Significance of the First Ten Days and Nights of Dhul Hijjah

Appendix 4 103
   Prayer and Sacrifice in `Eid Ul Adha (Feast of Sacrifice)

Appendix 5 105
   Complete the Sunnah of Qurban (Sacrifice)

ABOUT THE AUTHOR

PROFILE

For the past two decades, Mawlana Shaykh As-Sayed Nurjan Mirahmadi has worked hard to spread the true Islamic teachings of love, acceptance, respect and peace throughout the world and opposes extremism in all its forms. An expert on Islamic spirituality, he has studied with some of the world's leading Islamic scholars of our time.

Shaykh As-Sayed Mirahmadi has also founded numerous educational and charitable organizations. He has travelled extensively throughout the world learning and teaching Islamic meditation and healing, understanding the channeling of Divine energy, discipline of the self, and the process of self-realization. He teaches these spiritual arts to groups around the world, regardless of religious denomination.

BACKGROUND

Shaykh As-Sayed Nurjan Mirahmadi studied Business Management at the University of Southern California. He then established and managed a successful healthcare company and imaging centers throughout Southern California. Having achieved business success at a remarkably young age, Shaykh As-Sayed Nurjan Mirahmadi shifted his focus from the private sector to the world of spirituality. In 1994 he pursued his religious studies and devoted himself to be of service to those in need. He combined his personal drive and financial talents to work for the less fortunate and founded an international relief organization, a spiritual healing center, and a religious social group for at-risk youth.

In 1995, he became a protégé of Mawlana Shaykh Hisham Kabbani for in-depth studies in Islamic spirituality known as Sufism. He studied and accompanied Shaykh Kabbani on many tours and learned about Sufi practices around the world. Together with Shaykh Kabbani, he has established a number of other Islamic educational organizations and relief programs throughout the world.

Shaykh As-Sayed Nurjan Mirahmadi has received written *ijazas* (authorization) to be a Spiritual guide, from two of the World Leaders of the Nashbandi Nazimiya Sufi Order; Sultan al-Awliya Shaykh Muhammad Nazim al-Haqqani and Mawlana Shaykh Muhammad Hisham Kabbani. He is authorized to teach, guide, and counsel religious students around the world to Islamic Spirituality.

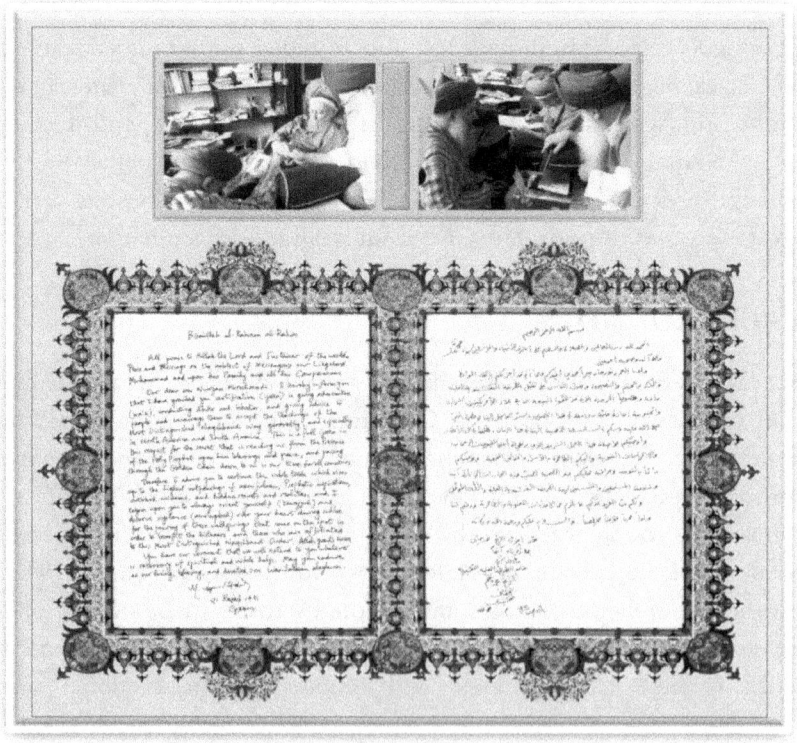

Shaykh As-Sayed Nurjan Mirahmadi has taught and travelled extensively throughout the world from Uzbekistan to Singapore, Thailand, Indonesia, Cyprus, Argentina, Peru, and North America. He teaches the spiritual sciences of Classical Islam, including meditation (*tafakkur*), subtle energy points (*lata'if*), Islamic healing, the secrets of letters and numbers (*ilm huroof*), disciplining the self (*tarbiyya*), and the process of self-realization (*ma'arifat*). He teaches the Muslim communities the prophetic ways of being kind, respectful and to live in harmony with people. He emphasizes on good manners and respect, and often reminds his students that the spiritual journey begins from within and "You can't give what you don't have."

ACCOMPLISHMENTS

One of Shaykh As-Sayed Nurjan's greatest accomplishments has been the worldwide dissemination of the spiritual teachings of Classical Islam through his books and online presence. The Prophet Muhammad (ﷺ) has told us, "Speak to people according to their levels." In an era of social media, Shaykh As-Sayed Nurjan's ability to reach a new generation of spiritual seekers through the Internet has been remarkable. His NurMuhammad.com website alone has over 1,000 unique visitors each day, and since its inception has seen more than 150,000 downloads of the book *"Dailal Khairat"*, 1,150,000 free downloads of *Naqshbandi Muraqabah*, and another 500,000 downloads of the *Naqshbandi Book of Devotions (Awrad)*, as well as many more articles. As of September 2015, his Facebook pages "Shaykh Sayed Nurjan Mirahmadi" and "Nur Muhammad" combined have over 200,000 likes. Furthermore, his YouTube Channel "The Muhammadan Way" has over 1 million views, and his Google page, "Shaykh Sayed Nurjan Mirahmadi" has over 2.7 million views.

Shaykh As-Sayed Nurjan Mirahmadi focuses on the worldwide social media presence working on ways to bring knowledge to all seekers around the world. In 2015 he launched an Online University called

SimplyIman.org, to spread these traditional Spiritual Islamic teachings even further and make it accessible to all seekers around the world.

For over 20 years, Shaykh As-Sayed Nurjan has dedicated his life to spreading the true Islamic teachings of love, acceptance, respect and peace. Shaykh As-Sayed Nurjan Mirahmadi has established several non-profit organizations since the early 1990s and over the past eight years, he has founded numerous educational and charitable organizations. In the Greater Vancouver region alone, he has established the following:

Ahle Sunnah wal Jama of BC – this organization is a resource for authentic content, books, and articles from the Quran & Sunnah from around the world. It works in collaboration with the well-known international organizations, Al Azhar University of Cairo, Dar al Ifta of Egypt and Islamic Supreme Council of North America.

Hub e Rasul ﷺ Conference – monthly Milad & Mehfil-e-Zikr events are organized and held throughout the Lower Mainland. The aim is to revive the teachings of the Quran and Sunnah by celebrating holy events in true Islamic spirit (Isra wal Miraj, Laylatul Bara, Laylatul Qadr, Milad un-Nabi etc.)

Naqshbandi Nazimiya Islamic Center of Vancouver – this Center is a place for people of all faiths and beliefs to attend weekly zikr programs (circles of remembrance) three times a week (Thursdays, Fridays, and Saturdays). Shaykh Nurjan teaches above and beyond the principles of Islam including the deep realities of *maqam al-iman* (belief) and *maqam al-ihsan* (excellence of character).

SMC – an outreach organization that spreads teachings to the Western audience including concepts such as meditation, charity, and reaches out to other faiths to increase peace, love, and acceptance in the interfaith environment.

Simply Iman Cloud University – an international online platform allowing people from around the world to pursue studies in various aspects of faith and spirituality from a classical Islamic perspective. Students have the opportunity to learn at their own pace and engage in an open dialogue with a teacher in real-time.

Fatima Zahraa Helping Hand – this charity organization runs a food program every two weeks which feeds more than 500 less fortunate people in the downtown eastside of Vancouver. It also collects clothing and non-perishable food items for the BC Muslim Food Bank and the Burnaby Homeless Shelter.

Shaykh As-Sayed Nurjan has also established an international presence through many social media outlets including:
- **FaceBook (Shaykh Nurjan Mirahmadi)** with over a quarter million likes
- **YouTube Channel (NurMir)** with over 300 videos
- **NurMuhammad.com**, a comprehensive website containing many resources covering the deep realities of classical Islam.

Shaykh As-Sayed Nurjan's sincere mission is to spread the love of Sayyidina Muhammad (ﷺ) throughout the city for our families and children. If you would like to be a shareholder in all these blessings we invite you to support our Center by any means possible. We hope to strengthen our efforts by joining our hands in raising the Honourable Flag of Sayyidina Muhammad (ﷺ).

UNIVERSALLY RECOGNIZED SYMBOLS

The following Arabic and English symbols connote sacredness and are universally recognized by Muslims:

The symbol *(AJ)* represents *Azza wa Jal*, a high form of praise reserved for God alone, which is customarily recited after reading or pronouncing the common name Allah, and any of the ninety-nine Islamic Holy Names of God.

The symbol ﷺ represents *sall Allahu 'alayhi wa salaam* (God's blessings and greetings of peace be upon the Prophet), which is customarily recited after reading or pronouncing the holy name of the Prophet Muhammad (ﷺ).

The symbol *(as)* represents *'alayhi 's-salam* (peace be upon him/her), which is customarily recited after reading or prouncing the sanctified names of prophets, Prophet Muhammad's (ﷺ) family members, and the angels.

The symbol *(ra)* represents *radi-allahu 'anh/ 'anha* (may God be pleased with him/her), which is customarily recited after reading or pronouncing the holy names of Prophet Muhammad's (ﷺ) Companions.

HAJJ IS 'ARAFAT

'Arafat's Secret is Hazrat Ismail *(as)* Maqam Ihsan/Perfection

There are some stories and some events that we read about in Holy Qur'an and if we think from just the physical aspect we say, "Okay *alhamdulillah* that happened for them but what do I do with that information in my daily life, and in my daily activities?" The *malakoot* and the heavenly realm of light and the world of Light are timeless. There must be a timeless reality in which there is every relevance for the soul and, my day to day, is to achieve and to be dressed by these realities.

Importance of Understanding Sayyidina Ibrahim's *(as)* Story

This refers to the entirety of the way of faith and the actions of the pilgrimage laid by Sayyidina Ibrahim *(as)*. To have a child by Sayyida Hajar and that child to not be accepted and then to have to move away and create a home and a location for Sayyida Hajar, or Hagar, depending upon who is pronouncing. And then the establishment of the Holy *Ka'bah* and the reflection of Divine Reality upon Earth; it means this location was established by Sayyidina Ibrahim *(as)*.

So understanding of that location, understanding that *tawaf*, and understanding that reality. Then to sit in that location, but yet not the *Ka'bah* there, where he dropped off his wife Sayyida Hajar at that location and said, "I have to go, I will be back." In her pursuit and desire for thirst, as she has a child and they needed water, she goes back and forth, back and forth, the reality of why she goes back and forth seven times, hits the dirt and *Zam Zam* comes. *Zam Zam* from the *Kawthar*. These are the rivers and realities of Paradise which Allah *(AJ)* wanted to open upon this *dunya*.

The Secret of 7 Tawaf

Then the life of the child that Sayyidina Ismail *(as)* is growing up, they say, 10 or 11 or 12 years old. Then now the entirety and reality of Hajj is based on this event because all of Hajj is Arafat.

We make *tawaf* around *Ka'bah*; why are we making 7 circumambulations around that reality? Why 7 Paradises, why 7 *lataif* (subtleties) of the heart? It means every *tawaf* is for our reality in every Paradise of Allah *(AJ)* and in between these seven Paradises may be infinite, but we must have a reality in each Paradise. Who knows himself will know his *Rabb* (Lord).

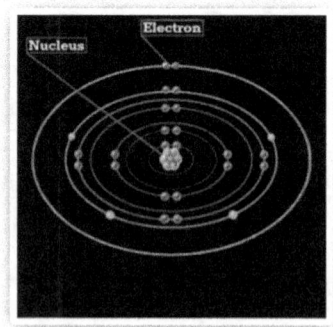

This means when we take a path of realization we begin to reflect inward. It means our journey from our outer form into our inner reality, is the reality of that *tawaf*. And how to keep moving in Allah's *(AJ)* Way, just like the atom that has seven rings. We are on the outermost ring trying to make our way towards that nucleus; there is a secret in those 7 *tawaf*.

Give That Which You Love the Most

But the child, Sayyidina Ismail *(as)* (from the story of Hajj), is that Sayyidina Ibrahim *(as)* begins to have a dream that Allah *(AJ)* says: Ya Ibrahim, you have given everything for Allah, and you are very generous. And this is very important in our life, because we give from our free will. It is nice to give from your free will. You want to give it, it comes to your heart and you give it. There is a lot of 'ourselves' in that giving because you determine when you are going to give it. So that comes from our will.

[Allah *(AJ)*] said: you have been generous but what Allah is commanding you is, We want that which you love dearer than your money and your property. All your life you prayed for that child to be born. That child is born, We want him. [Ibrahim *(as)*] said: "oh uh, I don't want to deal with that issue, I don't want to interfere with that." Allah *(AJ)* says: no, no put that on the table. Three times the image came; the dream came to sacrifice Ismail *(as)* and Sayyidina Ibrahim *(as)*, no I go to sleep, one, two, three. The third time he knew it is real, Allah *(AJ)* wants that sacrifice. Immediately he prepares himself, goes to the room to take Sayyidina Ismail *(as)* to *Jabal ar-Rahma* on Arafat for the sacrifice.

Sayyidina Ibrahim *(as)* Represents Perfection of the 'Form' Reality of Crescent and Star in Islam

It means that Sayyidina Ibrahim *(as)* is representing the 'form' and the perfection of form, which is why it is the *Nabi*. It means it is the example for us that we have to perfect our form. And it means that is the reality of the moon, when we show the crescent and the star. It is not like this (Shaykh shows crescent with horns upward), these represents the horns of Shaytan.

Secret Realities of Hajj

The crescent of the moon like that (sideways) and the star is the perfection of the soul, the *noor*. It means perfect your body, perfect the soul, as something is going to be born from that reality; these are the three realities.

Perfect Your Form By Following Sunnah

Sayyidina Ibrahim *(as)* represents for us, perfect your form. That is why you follow the *sunnah*. You follow the *Sunnah* of the prophets *(alayhi 's-salaat wa 's-salaam)* because they are the perfection of the form. They give you the Law, they give you the yes, the no, the do, and the don't. When you perfect that then we are understanding the reality that Sayyidina Ibrahim *(as)* wants for us to understand because the Hajj is the way of *iman* (faith) and the perfection of *imaan*. Our journeying 12 months to reach to this 12th month [*Dhul Hijja*]. The 12th month is the completion.

Ibrahim's *(as)* 3 Dreams, 3 Locks on the Heart, 3 Jamarat

Sayyidina Ibrahim *(as)* is describing that these three that came to me and the third time I acted upon it because there are also three locks upon the heart of the believer. The heart of the believer is locked where Allah *(AJ)* describes that their *qalb* has a lock upon their ears, has a lock upon their eyes and has a *kiswa* covering their heart. It means these have to be removed. That is why *jamarat* has 3 stones, the 3 times that Shaytan is attacking. Means he is waiting 3 times for a confirmation, but the body is struggling to submit to Allah *(AJ)*. That the order comes and this is a *Nabi*. Imagine in our lives, when you are given an order by the shaykh or given an order, you have 3 days to complete it. After 3 days it becomes stale, it becomes something that was not what was ordered and the co-ordinance begins to change.

Ibrahim *(as)* Representing Body

Allah *(AJ)* doesn't even give 3 days, but the minute he woke up, he didn't listen. He went back to sleep, again it came, woke up didn't listen. He went back to sleep, again it came. The third time was confirmation in one night, "get out; do what you have been ordered to do". Sayyidina Ibrahim *(as)* gets up and takes his son and begins to go towards the mountain, *Jabal ar-Rahma*.

Sayyidatina Hajar Represents Reality of Soul

Shaytan immediately goes to Sayyida Hajar, which is representing the wife, which is representing the reality of the soul mate. Your 'soul's mate' means the reality of his soul and her perfection of character. She was purchased, she had no free will. Even she represents that she was a captive, which is a polite word. She was captive, and she was turned into the wife of Sayyidina Ibrahim *(as)*, representing the soul in *tasleem*, in submission.

3 Attacks of Shaytan on Body, Soul, and....

1. Shaytan came to the body, tried to block Sayyidina Ibrahim *(as)*, so 3 times Allah *(AJ)* had to send *isharat* (sign), that get up, don't pass what Allah *(AJ)* is asking or you are going to be in big trouble. Immediately he gets up and begins to take his son to do what Allah *(AJ)* has commanded.

2. Then Shaytan goes to the soul, goes to Sayyida Hajar and says, "Do you know what Sayyidina Ibrahim is about to do?" and begins to describe. She said, "You don't have to describe to me, he is a *Nabiullah* (Prophet of Allah) and a *Rasulullah*, (Messenger of Allah). Whatever he has been commanded, *samina wa a`atana* (I heard and I obey)"; her faith in his belief and in his character made her to *tasleem*.

Secret Realities of Hajj

It means in our daily life this is the battle that we are facing. That my soul wants to believe and my body is constantly struggling. And my soul is telling me that, "I am not going to follow your body, until your body is in submission to Allah *(AJ)*. You are going to put harm upon me". And this becomes the perfection of character; this is the whole way of *ma'rifa*, of gnosticism, of realities.

In that timeless event, when we are seeing, because the Prophet of Allah *(AJ)* is the best of examples. [Ibrahim *(as)* saying] that my faith and my character was upright and *hanif*. And my wife realized that that character is true and whatever Shaytan came to tell her, [she said], "I am not listening. If Allah *(AJ)* has ordered him to do what you say Allah *(AJ)* has ordered, I am submitting." This is now the perfection of the soul.

Head vs. Heart
The Way of Reality is Not Through the Mind

Our whole way is that the soul is trying to submit, trying to listen, trying to understand, but doesn't have confidence in the body. That is why the *turuq* (Sufi paths) and the way of reality are not meant for the mind. You don't hear the Shaykh through the head and say that, "I don't understand." But it is meant to open your heart and allow them into the 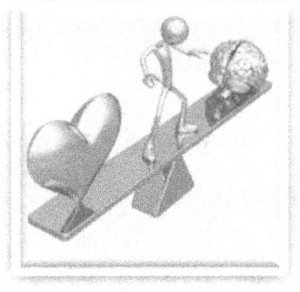 heart until their Light begins to enter into the heart. Because when you love somebody they enter into your heart. When you like someone, eh, he is okay, it is entered into the (shaykh points to the head). Because you constantly begin to analyze whatever the person is doing or saying, "Is it correct or is it not correct, is it like this or like that." This is where Shaytan is (shaykh points to the head) and all the *waswas*. This is not where they want the Light of Faith to enter. They want the Light of Faith to enter within the heart.

Open Your Heart With Love of Awliya

It means open your heart with *ishq* and *muhabbat*. Their light begins to enter into the heart. That is *atiullaha wa ati ar-rasul wa ulil amri minkum*.

The *ulul `amr*, the Light of their faith begins to enter into the heart of the believer. The love for them, that Light enters the heart and that Light begins to fight and begins to perfect faith! We don't have the ability to perfect it ourselves.

Qul in kuntum tuhibbuna Allah fattabi`ooni, from the *tabi'yeen* (the followers).

قُلْ إِنْ كُنْتُمْ تُحِبُّونَ اللَّـهَ فَاتَّبِعُونِيْ... ٣١

3:31 – *Qul in kuntum tuhibbon Allaha fattabi'onee,* ...*(Surat Al 'Imran)*

Say, [O Muhammad], "If you should love Allah, then follow me, [so] ... *(Family of Imran)*

Allah *(AJ)* is describing for us in Holy Qur'an: if you want My love, don't assume you have it, follow him. Follow who? Sayyidina Muhammad (ﷺ), and *ashaabin Nabi* (ﷺ), *Ahlul Bayt Nabi* (ﷺ), and what we call the *tabi'yeen, tabi'yeen, tabi'yeen, tabi'yeen,* all those who followed, those who followed, those who followed, and who did they follow? Sayyidina Muhammad (ﷺ) and they completed Allah's *(AJ)* order in Holy Qur'an:

Qul in kuntum tuhiboona fattabi'oonee, yuhbibkumullah...

$$\text{قُلْ إِن كُنتُمْ تُحِبُّونَ اللَّهَ فَاتَّبِعُونِي يُحْبِبْكُمُ اللَّهُ وَيَغْفِرْ لَكُمْ ذُنُوبَكُمْ ۗ وَاللَّهُ غَفُورٌ رَّحِيمٌ ٣١}$$

3:31 – Qul in kuntum tuhibbon Allaha fattabi'onee, yuhbibkumUllahu wa yaghfir lakum dhunobakum wallahu Ghaforur Raheem. (Surat Al 'Imran)

Say, [O Muhammad], "If you should love Allah, then follow me, [so] Allah will love you and forgive you your sins. And Allah is Forgiving and Merciful." (Family of Imran 3:31)

Shaytan Confuses the Head

Allah *(AJ)* says if you complete that, I am going to love you. If Allah's *(AJ)* Love comes, that is *Nur al-Imaan* (Light of Faith). It means they come into the heart, not into the head to analyze. The head carries no love. The head carries logic and even good and clear logic, because Shaytan can pirate the head but Shaytan cannot enter into the deep recesses of the heart. If that love becomes true and that love becomes pure, it goes so far deep; it overtakes full control of the authority of the body. But if you bring love into the head it's not really love. It is going to be constantly analyzing them, analyzing them, until Shaytan comes and begins to play with that television and begins to send different frequencies and your head is always confused.

The first *zikr* of all *turuq* is *laa ilaaha illallah*, [Shaykh moves head up with the word *laa* indicating 'nothing']. *Laa* means cut your head, *illaaha* (moves head to right side of chest) *illAllah* (moves head towards the heart). It means no head in this way. Head, you leave it for your school, for your education, for your money. The way of *imaan* is the way of the heart.

It means the soul is so purified that it accepts what Sayyidina Ibrahim *(as)* is bringing and he begins to take him for that reality. And Sayyida Hajar accepting that if this is what has been ordered, I am subjecting myself to the body. Now the body and and soul are in *tasleem* (palms together). Most are like this (palms perpendicular), the soul says, "Ah uh, you look like you are going to take us off the mountain, we are going to be killed by following you. We are going to be destroyed by following you." This becomes the 'ying' and 'yang', constant battle, constant battle, constant battle…

The concept of the *imam* is that you must apply someone greater than yourself, more pious than yourself, more honoured than yourself as your *imam*. By having the guide, by having the *ulul amr*, they are the *imam* of the family. So that the body understands and the soul understands, that you are of course from what the *imam* is saying. As soon as they begin to move and adjust themselves, the body is submitting, the soul is submitting, the perfection of that reality comes. And what is now born from men and women who come together in marriage? It is a child.

Ismail *(as)* – The Youthful Innocence and Perfection

Sayyidina Ismail *(as)* is the birth of that reality. That is why the *darajat* (rank) and the *maqam* (station) are so high. It means the birth of the perfection of the physicality, the perfection of the soul, is now the perfection of the *futuha (laa fatah illa `Ali)*, the *futuha* is what you call Islamic chivalry. The youthful innocent; that is a perfected innocence. It doesn't have the dirtiness of an adult, who already made many *ghunna*, many sins and trying to purify themselves.

What sets apart Sayyidina `Ali *(as)* is that from childhood, his perfection of submission, with no *ghunna* (sin), nothing wrong. His entire life was in *tasleem* and submission, his entire

life in the love of Sayyidina Muhammad (ﷺ). That is representing Sayyidina Ismail *(as)* that because my father has perfected his physicality, my mother representing the soul and her submission to his reality, because she is from his rib.

Where Prophet (ﷺ) describes but the ladies don't like to hear that: If I would have, I would have women to make *sajda* to their husband, because they come from him. Allah *(AJ)* created man from His Hand and breathed upon him and from the reality of that *insaan*, pulled out from the rib, is the reality of *Hawa* (Eve). But shows the perfection of relationship, that when that physicality is truly submitting and the confidence and the accommodation and the coordinance are correct, the soul is in *tasleem*. If the soul is in *tasleem*, Sayyidina Ismail *(as)* is born. Sayyidina Ismail *(as)* is in perfection.

'Arafat is About Sayyidina Ismail *(as)*

So as they are going up now, because all of Hajj is 'Arafat. 'Arafat is about Sayyidina Ismail *(as)*. Means with *tafakkur*, the dialogue that *awliya* asked, that when Sayyidina Ibrahim *(as)* was going up to sacrifice his son Sayyidina Ismail *(as)*, Sayyidina Ibrahim *(as)* was shaking, the smell of burning flesh was coming from the extent of the difficulty to make that choice. He laid Sayyidina Ismail *(as)* down. Sayyidina Ismail *(as)* told him, "*Yaa baba,* don't worry. With what Allah *(AJ)* has commanded you, *inshaAllah* you will find me to be patient."

Ismail *(as)* Represents *Muqamal Ihsan* – Station of Excellence

Maqaam al-Ihsaan, this is the station of *firasah* in which you pray and you see Allah *(AJ)*. Stop right there, because they explain that: if you don't see then Allah *(AJ)* sees you. But that is not Sayyidina Ismail *(as)*. Sayyidina Ismail *(as)* is seeing the Divinely Presence and understanding the order of a prophet of Allah *(AJ)*, of the six great prophets of Allah *(AJ)*. It means you are below the prophet, for you to have *isharat* (sign) of understanding what is coming to the Prophet (ﷺ). It is an example of a tremendous station in the Divinely Presence. That you will find me to be patient with what Allah *(AJ)* is ordering you, means he knows his own sacrifice is on the table. He knows that he is going to sacrifice himself for this *noor* Muhammad (ﷺ) that is coming. And that is the *azhimat* (greatness) of Sayyidina Muhammad (ﷺ).

Ismail *(as)* Sacrificed Himself – Lineage of Muhammad (ﷺ)

All of Hajj is 'Arafat. All of 'Arafat is the reality of Sayyidina Ismail *(as)*. *Yaa* Sayyidina Ibrahim *(as)*, you are going to sacrifice your property and a lot of burning, a lot of intensity, and a lot of fear. But Sayyidina Ismail *(as)* was sacrificing himself for Allah's *Rida* and satisfaction. From that light is the light of Sayyidina Muhammad (ﷺ). That is the reality of Sayyidina Muhammad (ﷺ).

When Prophet (ﷺ) comes on to this Earth, he is coming from that lineage to describe to us that: I am from those who would sacrifice ourselves for Allah *(AJ)*. We don't sacrifice properties and goods, this is not our interest. Our interest is to sacrifice ourselves for what Allah *(AJ)* wants from us.

Now *Ahl al-Bayt* begin to move in and they begin to teach. You have from 1 to 12 for regular people, for *awliyaullah* they are moving at a different reality. That twelfth month for *awliyaullah* is 12 times the reality of 9, because 9 is the *sultanat* of reality. That is 108 (12×9) and it is *Surat al-Kawthar*. From that immediately *awliyaullah* step in and begin to teach the *Ahl al-Bayt*. That Imam 'Ali *(as)* is teaching, every month one of these *imams* is in charge of that reality. The first one being *Muharram* being under the authority of Sayyidina `Ali *(as)* and the 12th month is under the authority of Sayyidina Mahdi *(as)*.

Reality of Imam Mahdi *(as)* and Sacrifice in Hajj

Muhammad al Mahdi *(as)* is the Muhammadan *hadi*, most guided soul of the Muhammadan Reality *(as)*. And why all the prophesied events of Sayyidina Mahdi *(as)* are initiated by Hajj? It means for the arrival of Sayyidina Mahdi *(as)* in all the *hadith* and all the scholars of *hadith* will tell you that there will be a tremendous battle at the time of Hajj with much bloodshed and many events will have transpired. At that time they will be waiting for Sayyidina Mahdi *(as)*. Why? Because the 12th month and the reality of the 12th *Imam*, and the reality of Hajj. All of them are an eternal reality. There is no one shot, it is eternal. It is not a coincidence that Sayyidina Mahdi *(as)* is in charge of the reality of that *tajjali* for Hajj. And that Hajj is based on 'Arafat and 'Arafat is based on sacrifice, and these are the *Ahl al-Kawthar*.

Bismillah ar-Rahman ar-Raheem. Inna `atayna ka 'l-kawthar, fasalli li-rabbika wanhar, inna sha'ni aka huwa 'l-abtar.

إِنَّا أَعْطَيْنَاكَ الْكَوْثَرَ (١) فَصَلِّ لِرَبِّكَ وَانْحَرْ (٢) إِنَّ شَانِئَكَ هُوَ الْأَبْتَرُ (٣)

108:1 – *Inna 'atayna kal kawthar*
108:2 – *Fasali li rabbika wanhar*
108:3 – *Inna shani-aka huwal abtar. (Surah al-Kawthar)*

*"To thee (O Muhammad) we have granted the Fount (of Abundance). (108:1)
So pray to your Lord and Sacrifice. (108:2)
Indeed, your enemy is the one cut off." (108:3) (The Abundance)*

It means if you want to be dressed by oceans of *Kawthar*, these are oceans of *hayaat*; they are the oceans of life, they are oceans of every Divine knowledge. *Fasalli rabbika wanhar*, that is the Arafat, "That to your Lord, sacrifice." So it means there must be the *ruhaniyaat* of Sayyidina Mahdi *(as)* on that Arafat. That the *Ahl al-Bayt* are present and the *Ahl al-Bayt* are inspiring within all the souls that are moving to Arafat, that you live a life of sacrifice, sacrifice yourself for Allah *(AJ)*. Now that is not to be confused with people who blow themselves up. So we have to say for every video because they may watch one video and not watch another video.

What Does Sacrifice Mean?

The way of sacrifice is to sacrifice yourself, your bad characteristics, your wants and your desires. You would never harm someone else, means your only harm is for yourself, that you can come against yourself, come against what you want, come against your desires. It means everything from what I want, *yaa Rabbi*, is not necessary, what is it that You want me to do, and I reach towards *tasleem* and submission? They are the masters of submission.

On that 'Arafat, they begin to describe: if it is Sayyidina Muhammad (ﷺ) you love and the reality of that Light that you love, take a path of sacrifice. That is why the *baab*, the gate in which they move, is based on 9. The 9th *surah* is *Surat at-Tawbah*, it has no *Bismillah ar-Rahmaan ar-Raheem*. They teach us and come into our lives that every year when it begins, enter into *tawbah*, where there is no *Bismillah ar-Rahmaan ar-Raheem* but make yourself to be *halal* for Allah *(AJ)*. Put your head on the table and say, *"Yaa Rabbi*, my desires, my wants, my needs are not important," because it is those same wants and desires that block us from everything. Whatever

Secret Realities of Hajj

Allah *(AJ)* wants from us of submission, we want something else! And this is blocking this *tasleem*, and submission. And they begin to teach, no, what Sayyidina Ibrahim *(as)* was bringing, if you want to reach the reality of Sayyidina Ismail *(as)*. It is represented by submission; it is represented by self sacrifice; that 'Arafat is the secret of the Light of Sayyidina Muhammad (ﷺ) coming into *dunya*. And that Prophet's (ﷺ) mission in life was to teach how to annihilate the self, to reach the Divinely Presence and satisfaction of Allah *(AJ)*.

We pray that not only the physical Hajj to be done, but more important is the spiritual Hajj. That Allah *(AJ)* accept from us and teach us how to bring the physical desire down. How to bring the power of the soul out so something truly new can be born. That new reality, if born, is something unimaginable of what it's been dressed with. Where people see you and don't recognize you as the one they knew before because it is an entire new reality that Allah *(AJ)* dressed the soul from.

Subhana rabbika rabil 'izzati 'ama yasifoon, Wa salamun 'alal mursaleen wal hamdulillahi rabbil 'alameen. Bi hurmati Muhammadil Mustafa wa bi siratil suratil Fatiha.

REALITY OF HAJJ

Everything Makes Tawaf (Circumambulation) From Atom to Adam to Planets

Alhamdulillah from Mawlana Shaykh's teaching that we are now entering the holy month of *Dhul Hijjah* and in the beginning of the Hajj, and the pilgrimage towards the Divinely Presence. That is symbolic by the Hajj and the twelfth month and the completion of the journey toward the movement of Divinely Presence. And everything of the realities of Islam is the realities of the Heavens. The realities of nature and everything around us shows us proof of what Prophet (ﷺ) brought for humanity. That is its greatness that you can't have something that only you say it to be true and nothing around you confirms that.

The greatness of Sayyidina Muhammad (ﷺ) is that he brings for us a religion with its laws, its rituals, its teachings and you see all of its reality in nature in its natural form of submission that Allah *(AJ)* wants for us the same.

Everything Must Circumambulate That Which is Supreme

The importance of Hajj from Mawlana Shaykh's teaching, is one of many oceans of reality, is that *tawaf* and circumambulation and the symbolic presence of the Divinely Presence. It is a symbol in our life that the Light is supreme, the Lord is supreme, Allah *(AJ)* is supreme. And everything must circumambulate that which is supreme. That which is false and imitated, it must move around and circumambulate that which is true, what we call *Haqq*, the Reality.

It means then when you watch the *tawaf* of *Ka`bah* it is symbolic, and everything around us will show that reality. So we look at the *tawaf*, and it is symbolized by the heart, it is symbolized by the Divinely Presence. We come into that reality, asking to lose our identity, to strip away our clothing that identifies us from wealth, from status, from everything. We take away everything and you put two sheets of cloth and you circumambulate what is symbolic of the Divinely Presence. Nobody believes the house to be Allah's *(AJ)* Presence. It is a *tajjali* and manifestation that unifies humanity and reminds our humanity that: I am not independent and I am dependent on my Creator. And from my creator comes all powers, all energies, all realities, and I am merely a manifestation. And I am circumambulating saying, "*Labbayk, allahuma labbayk* لبيك الهم لبيك, I have heard Your call and I am coming." Everything in nature shows us that reality.

Earth Circumambulates Around the Sun

You can say,"O, I am not Muslim, and I am not going to do that," and

Allah *(AJ)*, doesn't mind, doesn't care, doesn't matter because being Muslim is not a name and is not a noun. It's not a label, but it means one who submits. They teach us

that look at the Earth, all of us are making a Hajj; because the Earth is making *tawaf* around the Sun. So if you want to go for Hajj or if you don't want to go for Hajj, it doesn't matter. But when you look back and see my Earth is circumambulating the Sun and you are making a *tawaf* around the Sun. You are now making a Hajj because the Sun is symbolic of Light and the Light is eternal.

It is the same Sun that was for Nabi Musa (Moses) *(as)*, and was for Sayyidina Adam *(as)*. It was the Light and the Light has always been and we came and went. We lived a few years on this Earth, we built a few structures and all of them went, and the Sun is still there. It means it was symbolic, that your Earth is making *tawaf*, it is circumambulating My Divinely Majesty. You need that Sun to eat, you need that Sun to breathe; without the Sun and photosynthesis you have no air. Without that Sun you have no sight. It means every vegetation and every food, and every breath we take is from that. Then Allah *(AJ)* says: make *tawaf*, and ordered the Earth, you make a circumambulation, to show who is the majestic one. It is the Sun. It has a supremacy over the Earth and the Earth makes its *tawaf*. Then Allah *(AJ)* is describing in Holy Qur'an: *We will show you every sign from the horizon and within yourselves.*

سَنُرِيهِمْ آيَاتِنَا فِي الْآفَاقِ وَفِي أَنفُسِهِمْ حَتَّىٰ يَتَبَيَّنَ لَهُمْ أَنَّهُ الْحَقُّ ۗ ... ٥٣

41:53 – Sanureehim ayatina fil afaqi wa fee anfusihim hatta yatabayyana lahum annahu alhaqqu, …(Surat Al Isra)

"We will show them Our signs in the horizons and within themselves until it becomes clear to them that it is the truth…" (The Night Journey 41:53)

Electrons Are Making *Tawaf* Around the Nucleus

The greatness of Islam, the greatness of what Prophet (ﷺ), brought is that every sign will be visible outside and inside ourselves. So we look at the *tawaf* and we realize that the Earth is making *tawaf*. Then

Secret Realities of Hajj

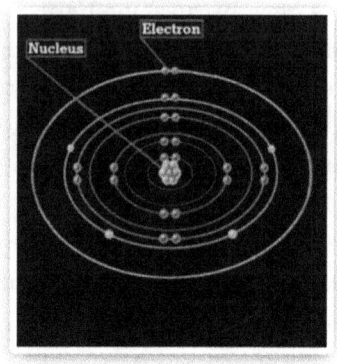

they begin to teach as soon as you take eighth or ninth grade Physics, that all your electrons are making *tawaf* around the nucleus, the nucleus being the center of power and only one; 'atom' or 'Adam' is the same. It doesn't matter if it was small or if it became something big, and called him ADAM. But the reality is just one atom, of that Adam, it has the same reality. It has seven layers and all the electrons represent negativity, that which is 'false and that which is perishing.'

وَ قُلْ جَآءَالْحَقُّ وَزَهَقَ الْبَطِلُ، إِنَّ الْبَطِلَ كَانَ زَهُوقًا

17:81 – *Wa qul jaa alhaqqu wa zahaqal baatil, innal batila kana zahooqa.* (Surat Al Isra)

"And say, Truth has come, and falsehood has departed. Indeed is falsehood, [by nature], ever bound to depart." (The Night Journey 17:81)

They circumambulate the center, the nucleus, and the nucleus represents the 'power'. The nucleus represents the goal, the source of energy, the source of all realities, emanating. And what makes the electrons to circumambulate is the power of the nucleus. We exist because of that circumambulation.

Three Forces of Atoms – Reality of Our Existance

It means if the ego wants to make pilgrimage, or not, Allah *(AJ)* doesn't care, but if you look around you see the Earth making its pilgrimage. We see our internal reality; its existence is based on that concept. Your electrons are circumambulating because of the force and the attraction to the center. If there was no attraction to the nucleus, which is the Divinely Presence, the electrons would not move; they would stand and drop. It is their love for the center, their desire to unite and move to the center, which creates now the attraction. A powerful attraction that it now wants to come, and Allah *(AJ)* doesn't give permission, and it begins now the movement and the circumambulation.

It means there are **three forces;** 'mass attraction', 'circumambulation', and 'upward thrust' are the reality of our entire existence.

1. Mass attraction – Love
2. Circumambulation – Follow
3. Upward thrust – Levitate

All your electrons, in love with the center, the nucleus, because of that attraction they are beginning to circumambulate. Anything that circumambulates at the speed in which the electrons are circumambulating, they begin to forget why they are circumambulating and begin to levitate. So they love, and they begin to follow and then third, they are levitating.

Reality of Hologram As Our Existence

Why do we have a hologram as an existence? All science came and said we are holograms. Your atoms are just moving very fast and giving the appearance of something solid. And that's all because of love. If that love was taken away, the electron would not circumambulate. If the electron did not circumambulate, there would be no form. There would be no circumambulation, there would be no existence. It means Allah *(AJ)* created this Creation out of Divinely Love.

Allah *(AJ)* Created the Creation Out of Love

So we learn that our smallest reality is existing in that *tawaf*. We see the outward people making that *tawaf*. We see the planet making the *tawaf*. This is what Allah *(AJ)* and Prophet (ﷺ) brought for us. That you see all My Signs upon the horizon and you see it within yourself.

سَنُرِيهِمْ آيَاتِنَا فِي الْآفَاقِ وَفِي أَنفُسِهِمْ حَتَّىٰ يَتَبَيَّنَ لَهُمْ أَنَّهُ الْحَقُّ ۗ ... ٥٣

41:53 – Sanureehim ayatina fil afaqi wa fee anfusihim hatta yatabayyana lahum annahu alhaqqu, …(Surat Al Isra)

"We will show them Our signs in the horizons and within themselves until it becomes clear to them that it is the truth…" (The Night Journey 41:53)

The Reality of Islam is Submission

The reality of Islam is not someone's crazy interpretation. The reality of Islam is the reality of submission. The reality of the Divinely Presence is the reality of submission to the Divinely Love, which loves everything, which nurtures everything, which cares for everything. We are on this Earth for love. We are on this Earth to find our reality. We are not on the Earth to harm anyone; we are not on the Earth to judge anyone. If anything, the only one we should judge is ourselves: is Allah *(AJ)* going to be happy with me or not?

Then the Hajj opens up a tremendous reality of everything that is based on circumambulation. You circumambulate that which you love. It means even your attendance and coming for *majlis* of *zikr* is based on love. If we don't love it, we don't come. And when we come, it is an expression of love and you grow.

It means the love brings you. If you are constantly moving in that love you find your elevation and spiritual growth. Whether it is the hologram of the physicality or whether it is the *Mi`raj* of the soul, moving to the Divinely Presence, it is based on love. It has such an attraction for the Divinely Presence, the soul is moving to be in the nucleus; not stuck with the world of form and playing only with the form.

We Are All Born in Submission

Then Mawlana Shaykh begins to describe that even when you look within yourself, because what they want us to understand is that we are all born Muslim. We are all born in submission. Don't be lost by Arabic words. Bring it back to the language that you speak and you understand; it is that your entire being was born in submission. From the atoms within your soul, within your body submit, and every day they submit. The Earth submits. Everything submits except my ego, and that's the one Allah *(AJ)* says you should be destroying that one, the one that is constantly coming against My Divinely Presence. But everything about our nature shows that it is in *tasleem*, in submission, submitting to the Will of Allah *(AJ)* and that is why:

"*Thy kingdom come*", 'Thy' Kingdom, not 'your' kingdom or 'my' kingdom, 'Thy Kingdom' "on Earth as it is in Heaven." It means *tasleem*, and submit. Submit to My Kingdom, My Kingdom governs everything. But only Mankind, you are *jahool*, you are ignorant. Allah *(AJ)* calls us in Holy Qur'an: Mankind is ignorant. I offered these realities to the mountains, they said, 'no'. I offered to all of creation and they said 'no'. But only mankind said, "I will take it" because they didn't understand the extent of the reality and how they are going to be accountable to Allah *(AJ)*.

إِنَّا عَرَضْنَا الْأَمَانَةَ عَلَى السَّمَاوَاتِ وَالْأَرْضِ وَالْجِبَالِ فَأَبَيْنَ أَن يَحْمِلْنَهَا وَأَشْفَقْنَ مِنْهَا وَحَمَلَهَا الْإِنسَانُ ۖ إِنَّهُ كَانَ ظَلُومًا جَهُولًا ٧٢

33:72 – Inna a'radnal amanata 'alas Samawati wal ardi wal jibali, fa abayna an yahmilnaha wa ashfaqna minha wa hamalaha al Insanu, innahu kana zhaloman jahoola. (Surat Al Ahzab)

"Indeed, we offered the Trust to the heavens and the earth and the mountains, and they declined to bear it and feared it; but man [undertook to] bear it. Indeed, he was unjust and ignorant." (The Combined Forces 33:72)

That is why everything in nature submits. Everything in nature shows its complete submission.

First Hajj Was in the Womb

Then they say even look closer, how did you get on this Earth? When your baba met your mama. How did you come on to this Earth? Your mom has a womb that is called a *haramain* (sacred sanctity). The

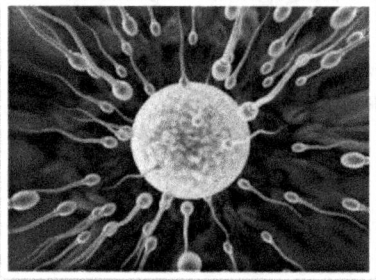

womb, no *haram* is allowed in the womb; that is why we are not allowed to show the belly of a woman because it is the *haramain*. There should be no *haram* in that womb; it carries the secret of life. Allah *(AJ)* drops one *Ka'bah*, one egg drops into the womb, it is a *Ka`bah*. *Ka`bah* is one, the nucleus is one, no many gods and multiple gods; *laa shareek* (No partner), it is one. The oneness of egg is dropped into the womb which is the Makkah, no *haram*.

That one egg comes and the male releases 500,000, or whatever it is. There are a lot of *hajjis* released into the *haramain*.

$$ ثُمَّ جَعَلْنَاهُ نُطْفَةً فِي قَرَارٍ مَّكِينٍ ١٣ $$

23:13 – Thumma ja'alnahu Nutfatan fi qararin Makeen. (Surat al Muminoon)

"Then We placed him as a sperm-drop in a firm lodging." (The Believers 23:13)

If you watch under the microscope on YouTube those *hajjis*, they shine with a white light. They show them moving around the egg exactly like you have an aerial footage of the *Ka'bah*.

Allah *(AJ)* wants to remind us: why you became so big? Didn't you come from this fluid that by its nature is dirty and you have to wash.

$$\text{أَلَمْ نَخْلُقكُّم مِّن مَّاء مَّهِينٍ}$$

77:20 – Alam Nakhluqukkum min maa in Maheen. (Surat al Mursalat)
"Have We not created you from a fluid (held) despicable (despised)?"
(The Emissaries 77:20)

When you look with the microscope, that image is just like watching the *tawaf* of the *Ka'bah*, because there is no more color, there is just

these white clothes and people moving. Then you look again at the microscope and the images from YouTube, and they are all fighting to kiss the black stone.

It means the one seed that comes in to the egg; it becomes the one whom Allah *(AJ)* is going to grant the secret of life. It means we made a Hajj in our mom's womb. We are the ones who won that ticket. We described that seven or eight years ago and a reminder for ourselves that we are the ones that won. We had 499,999 brothers and sisters that didn't make it. I was the one who Allah *(AJ)* granted my Hajj to be real, and my seed went into the egg. And Allah *(AJ)* granted that egg: you are now going to be granted a life. Come out and have an existence but remember where you came from, you came from that Hajj.

Secret Realities of Hajj

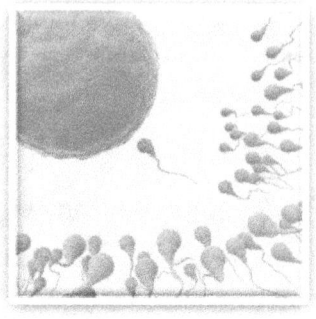

Everything around you shows that Hajj. Why is it that you grow up and become a renegade to My submission and say, "I am no longer going to make *tawaf* around You? I am no longer going to listen to You. I am no longer going to submit to You?" That is the only reason why Allah *(AJ)* sent the prophets, to remind: didn't you come from this Hajj? Isn't everything around you based on this Hajj? So then submit yourself and make your intention for Hajj.

أَوَلَمْ يَرَ الْإِنسَانُ أَنَّا خَلَقْنَاهُ مِن نُّطْفَةٍ فَإِذَا هُوَ خَصِيمٌ مُّبِينٌ

36:77 -Awalam yaral Insanu anna khalaqnahu min Nutfatin fa idha huwa khaseemun mubeen. (Surat Yaseen)

"Does not man see that it is We Who created him from a sperm-drop? Yet behold! He (stands forth) as an open disputer!" (Yasin 36:77)

And everything around us should show that reality. And every reality the Prophet (ﷺ) brought and revealed through Holy Quran, has a sign within ourselves and upon the horizon. Upon the horizon is easier to see versus seeing the reality within ourselves. The reality within ourselves requires a *firasat* and a vision, that we be true and honest with ourselves and we see that reality.

We pray that this holy month opening *inshaAllah* on Saturday night or Sunday night depending upon where people are, that Allah *(AJ)* dress us from that reality. Bless us from the realities of Hajj, bless us from the reality of our first Hajj that brought us here.

Yaa Rabbi (O our Lord), You brought us through that Hajj, put us onto this Earth, now save us. Protect us from difficulty, protect us from wrong. Keep us under Your guidance and the intercession of

Sayyidina Muhammad (ﷺ), under the love of Sayyidina Muhammad (ﷺ), under the love and *nazar* of *awliya*. And that we return back to Your Divinely Presence with our Hajj being completed and our submission, *inshaAllah*, trying to complete it to the best of our ability.

Subhana rabbika rabil 'izzati 'ama yasifoon, Wa salamun 'alal mursaleen wal hamdulillahi rabbil 'alameen. Bi hurmati Muhammadil Mustafa wa bi siratil suratil Fatiha.

REALITY OF TAWAF (CIRCUMAMBULATION)

K'abah is the Heart of the Believers
Madina is the House of Allah

Allah *(AJ)*, in Holy Quran says, I am going to teach you within yourself and upon the horizons. You will see My signs upon the horizons and you will see My signs within yourself.

سَنُرِيهِمْ آيَاتِنَا فِي الْآفَاقِ وَفِي أَنفُسِهِمْ حَتَّىٰ يَتَبَيَّنَ لَهُمْ أَنَّهُ الْحَقُّ ۗ (٥٣)

41:53 – Sanureehim ayatina fil afaqi wa fee anfusihim hatta yatabayyana lahum annahu alhaqqu, …(Surat Al Isra)

"We will show them Our signs in the horizons and within themselves until it becomes clear to them that it is the truth…" (The Night Journey 41:53)

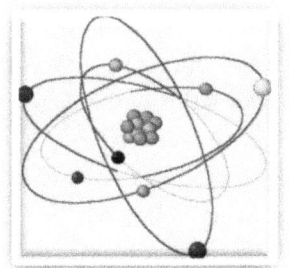

It means the way of *tafakkur* and contemplation is that there must be a reality within me and there must be a reality that Allah *(AJ)* is showing upon the horizons. If we don't understand the secret of *tawaf*, then we do not truly understand what Allah *(AJ)* wants from us. The *tawaf* is the circumambulation of

Secret Realities of Hajj

the holy *Ka'bah*. It means for us it is a deep reality. We find out now within ourselves, that our whole holographic image is based on this reality. **The whole of our being is based on love.** That love, the scientific and reality of love; not the love of lust and people jumping on each other. This is the divinely love, in which the divinely presence grants to our smallest being, our elements, our electrons. **The nucleolus of our being is the center of love.** If you don't understand the smallest, you don't know what you are doing. It is like you are going around the rocks and stones and become idol worshippers, *astaghfirullah* (asking for forgiveness). There must be a reality that a believer must have to understand within their heart. Before I can truly sometimes understand, I have to reflect within. Now *alhamdullilah* (praise be to Allah), they are teaching us from our atoms.

The atom circumbulates the nucleus. Why is it circumambulating the nucleus? Why do we have the whole hologram of our being based on that love? It means the Divine put within the nucleus a divinely love, an attraction; what they call mass attraction. It is such a powerful attraction that the outer elements want to collide; they want to go in to the nucleus. As a result Allah *(AJ)* creates a slight gentle force. There is a strong nuclear force and a weak force. That weak force is just enough to slightly push. If it was any stronger and hit, then the holographic image will be non-existant because it will send your love away. There's enough strength that your love gets into the nucleus and Allah *(AJ)* is not giving permission. Therefore, now you begin to look for another way. When the love is there, you are not stopping, so your elements don't stop.

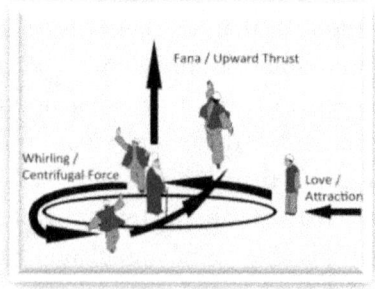

The mass attraction they describe like this; from the circumference your elements want to come to the nucleus. They are attracted by their very being. They have to be into the nucleus because of love, divinely love, a pure, sweet and innocent love. As a result, the electrons don't stop, they have no ego. No ego is telling them that, no go away, this is not for us. The electrons move because of the love, like a magnet it pulls. They move, they move, they keep moving to find a way in. They want to be in the nucleus.

It means the electrons; they begin the reality of *tawaf*. They are going around looking for a way to collide with the center. They want to reach the divinely presence or the symbol of divinely presence because, there is nothing like the divinely presence. It's a divinely light, divinely *qudrat* (power). Later they describe what that light is. It means that the electrons and the elements want to and they begin to move. As a result of their yearning and their love, they are moving to the center, moving to the center. They begin the circumambulation, they begin the *tawaf* (circumambulation), they begin the *tawaf*, and they begin the *tawaf*. And because they have no ego, they are lost within that love.

Then they begin the centrifugal force. It is the force that creates the spin. As a result of the love, there is a spin. The spin is so great and that's the whole reality of this creation. It's spinning at such a speed; it has forgotten why it's spinning. It forgot that it's lost in that love. As a result, it's an upward thrust. The attraction, the spin, and now the upward movement.

The attraction + the spin = the upward movement

All the atoms are moving and spinning at a rate of speed that is not comprehensible for us. The vastness of our creation, the vastness of our electrons; all are spinning out of divinely love, giving us an appearance. Allah *(AJ)* says, this life is but an illusion.

...وَمَا الْحَيَاةُ الدُّنْيَا إِلَّا مَتَاعُ الْغُرُورِ (١٨٥)

3:185 – … wa mal alhayatu addunya illa mata'u alghuroor. (Surat Ali Imran)

"*...And what is the life of this world except the enjoyment of delusion.*" (Family of Imran)

Scientists say yes, all of it is an illusion. If the spin stops, it collapses to nothingness. It collapses to something not as great as the sizes that we are seeing. That is the reality of love and that is the reality of our being. Allah *(AJ)* says everything is in my praise. Everything is in existence out of that divinely love.

تُسَبِّحُ لَهُ السَّمَاوَاتُ السَّبْعُ وَالْأَرْضُ وَمَن فِيهِنَّ ۚ وَإِن مِّن شَيْءٍ إِلَّا يُسَبِّحُ بِحَمْدِهِ وَلَـٰكِن لَّا تَفْقَهُونَ تَسْبِيحَهُمْ ۗ إِنَّهُ كَانَ حَلِيمًا غَفُورًا (٤٤)

17:44 – *Tusabbihu lahus samawatus sab'u wal ardu wa man feehinna wa in min shayin illa* **yusabbihu bihamdihi** *wa lakin la tafqahoona tasbeehahum innahu kana haleeman ghafoora. (Surat Al Isra)*

"The seven heavens and the earth and whatever is in them exalt Him. And **there is not a thing except that it exalts [Allah] by His praise**, *but you do not understand their [way of] exalting. Indeed, He is ever Forbearing and Forgiving." (The Night Journey 17:44)*

Planets Make *Tawaf* طواف (Circumambulation) Around the Sun

Then we find the earth spin around the sun. It's not *shirk*! But, the sun is the symbol of divinely light. Which is greater? The sun or the light of Sayyidina Muhammad (ﷺ). It's not comparable. The light of the prophetic souls, far out does any imaginary light of the sun because it's all within the bound of creation. Allah *(AJ)* says, this creation is not like a wing of mosquito for me, in value.

Sahi Ibn Sa'd (ra) reported that Allah's Messenger (ﷺ) said,
"*... in Allah's sight the world had so much worth as the wing of a mosquito,.*"
[Tirmidhi (4/560)]

It begins to teach us that everything is in *tawaf* (circumambulation) around the light. The planets make *tawaf* around the sun. They used to think before that the sun makes *tawaf* around the earth. But no, **the physical must make *tawaf* around the spiritual, the light. The light is eternal**. And all the planets on them are making *tawaf* around the sun. And everyone on the planet is making *tawaf* around the sun.

وَهُوَ الَّذِي خَلَقَ اللَّيْلَ وَالنَّهَارَ وَالشَّمْسَ وَالْقَمَرَ ۚ كُلٌّ فِي فَلَكٍ يَسْبَحُونَ (٣٣)

21:33 – Wa Huwal lazee khalaqal laila wannahaara washshamsa wal qamara kullun fee falakiny yashbahoon. (Surat Al-Anbiya)

"And He (is) The One Who created the night and the day, and the sun and the moon, each swimming in an orbit." (The Prophets 21:33)

They begin to teach us, look at the greater reality. You like it or you don't like it, Allah *(AJ)* is making you to make *tawaf* around the sun. Because Allah *(AJ)* is showing the *azzimat*, the greatness of His greatness. Study the sun. Not to worship the sun because, *tawaf* is an expression of love. Worship is our *salat*, (prayers) and acknowledging the divinely presence and praying to the divinely presence.

These are the *ayats* (signs) and *isharats* of the divinely light, divinely creation. Study the sun, and see that your breath is coming from the sun, through photosynthesis. Your vision is coming from the spectrum of light that you can see from the sun. Our whole existence on this planet is from the sun. As a result of respect and *ihtram* (respect), Allah *(AJ)* makes the earth to go around the sun. Be thankful and say *shukur* (thanks) to me and be thankful to my creation that I give you. **All planets begin to circumambulate the sun out of their thankfulness** because Allah's *(AJ)* *'izzat* (honor) and Allah's *(AJ)* might and power is in that reality. Allah *(AJ)* wants good character. He says, be thankful for what I am giving you.

We said before, which is greater? When you study the sun, you say all of that is coming from the magnificence of the sun. But, the

Secret Realities of Hajj

magnificence of Allah *(AJ)* is the power upon that sun. Your breathing, eating, and all your abilities come from that. We said which is greater, the sun or the light of Prophet (ﷺ)? The light of Prophet (ﷺ) is greater. Now how much do you owe the reality of Prophet (ﷺ)? If the sun is doing that for you, imagine the reality of where that sunlight is coming from.

These are the *sir* (secrets) of *Lam Jalala*. Everything must come from the secret of *la ilaha ilAllah* and goes directly to *Muhammadun RasulAllah* and comes out. This is for us the reality of *tawheed* and oneness. This is what Allah *(AJ)* is showing that for my *'izzat* to appear, it must be appearing through the reality of Prophet (ﷺ) and the prophetic reality of all the prophets. They carry that reality. Their lights far out shine that sun. Once we begin to understand how many blessings we get from the sun, how many nourishments we get from all of that. Allah *(AJ)* says, just you think then what are you getting from the reality of the souls of whom I love. My light is upon their hearts.

Now begins to open the reality of *tawaf*. When we understand the micro-reality of our being it is moving in this love. We are in a hologram of that love. If for any moment the electron stops its love, it collapses. We cease to exist.

Yusabihu bi hamdeh.

تُسَبِّحُ لَهُ السَّمَاوَاتُ السَّبْعُ وَالْأَرْضُ وَمَن فِيهِنَّ ۚ وَإِن مِّن شَيْءٍ إِلَّا يُسَبِّحُ بِحَمْدِهِ وَلَٰكِن لَّا تَفْقَهُونَ تَسْبِيحَهُمْ ۗ إِنَّهُ كَانَ حَلِيمًا غَفُورًا (٤٤)

17:44 – Tusabbihu lahus samawatus sab'u wal ardu wa man feehinna wa in min shayin illa yusabbihu bihamdihi wa lakin la tafqahoona tasbeehahum innahu kana haleeman ghafoora. (Surat Al Isra)

"The seven heavens and the earth and whatever is in them exalt Him. And there is not a thing except that it exalts [Allah] by His praise, but you do not understand their [way of] exalting. Indeed, He is ever Forbearing and Forgiving."
(The Night Journey 17:44)

Allah *(AJ)* says for verily everything is in my praise, in resonance, in an atomic resonance. Their atoms are resonating. It means they are singing. Now they have a technology that they can hear the earth sing. All spiritual masters teach; they can hear the planets. Everything has a frequency; the wood has a frequency, the glass has a frequency, the earth puts out a frequency, the planets and the sun put out a frequency. It means they are making a *dhikr*.

Ka'bah is the Heart of the Believers

Then Prophet (ﷺ) begins to teach, that nothing in the earth and nothing in the heaven can contain Allah *(AJ)* but the heart of the believer. From the Hadith Qudsi that Allah *(AJ)* says:

ما وسعني ارضي و لا سمايئ ولاكن وسعني قلب عبدي المؤمن ۞

"Maa wasi`anee ardee wa laa samayee wa laakin wasi`anee qalbi `abdee al-mu'min."

"Neither My Earth nor My Heavens can contain Me, but the heart of my Believing Servant." (Hadith Qudsi)

He is not talking about me and you. He is talking about the prophetic reality. **Qalbil Mumin baytullah** قلب المؤمن بيت الله **(Heart of the Believer is House of Allah).** It is very easy. This is a truth in plain sight. The best truth is hidden in plain sight because people think, no it has to be more complicated than that. No! The heart of the believer is the house of God. Divine says there is nothing up there that is going to hold Me and there is nothing down here that is going to hold Me. But **the heart of My believer is My house.** It means I reside, my *'izzat*, my might resides within that but not for you and me. Not now.

This is towards the understanding of greatness of the prophetic reality. When we go to the *ka'bah* and say *ya rabbi* (oh my lord) but the hadith is *qalbil mu'min baytullah*, now I am facing *baytullah* (Allah's house), there must be the **Qalb e Mumin (Heart of the Believer).** Why are you guys making it difficult?

The *qalbil mu'min*. Who are we talking about? It is the heart of the Prophet (ﷺ). Allah *(AJ's)* only concern is Prophet's (ﷺ) reality. That the *qalb* (heart) of Sayyidina Muhammad (ﷺ) is My house. And if you arrive at His house, who is there? The *Mu'min* (believer)! It's the *rohaniyat* of Sayyidina Muhammad (ﷺ). **Because of** the *rohaniyat* (spirituality) of Sayyidina Muhammad (ﷺ), Allah *(AJ)* sends His *tajali* (light). Why, you think Allah *(AJ)* sends

His *tajali* on the bricks so the bricks will be holy or the water and the cement? Or they think maybe the *khiswa*, the fabric is holy. They cut it (*khiswa*) up every year and sell it for billions of dollars to everybody who believes. Allah *(AJ)* is sending all that *tajali* on a fabric?

There must be something there that every *mu'min*, needs. Because the rules of paradise are that when you move to paradise, you can never be taken out of paradise. There must be a paradise light there. There must be *rohaniyat* of Prophet (ﷺ) there. As a result, all the real *mu'min* (believers), all the real *mukhlis* (sincere); Allah *(AJ)* puts a drop of their *arwah* (souls), drop of their souls; just even an atom is enough. That atom is enough to reflect back to their physicality or to their souls, wherever their souls are in *barzakh* (Purgatory) or in *dunya* (material world). Because one atom is as if all the atoms are there.

All those lights and all those atoms must be at the holy *ka'bah* because, this is the *hadith*. *Qalbil mu'min baytullah*. Now I came to the *baytullah*; where are the *mu'min*? As a result of that, Allah *(AJ)* says, you make *tawaf* طواف. Weren't you making *tawaf* around the sun? Which was better? You had no choice in the *tawaf* طواف around the sun; you sit on the earth. You can't say no put on the brake, I am not going to make *tawaf* around the sun. Allah *(AJ)* is showing you that light, you have *ihtram* (respect), you have respect. Sit on the *ard* (earth) and go around the *Shams* (sun). We have no choice. The earth makes a *tawaf* around the sun at the speed of 6,700 miles/hour.

They begin to teach, there must be very holy souls residing in *ka'bah*. That's what brings Allah's *nazar* (gaze) and *tajali* (light). As a result, their souls inside the *ka'bah*, they are making *tawaf* around Allah *(AJ)*. Because the reality of their souls, the heart within their souls; inside there is making *tawaf* around Allah *(AJ)*. Just like the Sun is making a very slow *tawaf*. It is making a *tawaf* to the *'izzat* that it is dressed by. The earth makes a *tawaf* all the way to the Pluto but, they keep the Pluto out. But, they keep the 9th planet out. Whatever it is, that entire galaxy and universe are all making a *tawaf*.

They begin to open the reality of that *tawaf*. That is reality of the light that resides in the holy *ka'bah*. It must be the light of very purified and blessed souls. As a result of their lights, Allah's *(AJ) nazar* (gaze) and *tajali* (light) is upon them. They are making *tawaf* around Allah *(AJ)* and the *jama'a* (group of people) on the outside is making *tawaf* around them. That's why Allah *(AJ)* wants you to pray in the *jama'a* because He doesn't care about your prayer. He cares about the prayer of the *Imam*. The *Imam* recites, he carries the *jama'a* behind. If the *imam* is bad, the prayer is off somewhere else. Allah *(AJ)* is showing us that for the sake of that holy light, My *nazar* (gaze), My dressing, and My blessing is upon that region. As a result, you come by imitation and make a *tawaf* to be dressed by the lights that those holy souls are already being dressed in.

Lam jalala. This is an active state of reality of Prophet's (ﷺ) soul. It's active because *qalbil mumin baytullah* and everybody is coming to receive those lights from the Prophet (ﷺ), from the lights of all the souls of all the *mu'min* (believers), from *Ashabin nabi* (ﷺ) (Prophet's companions), *ahlul bayte Nabi* (ﷺ) (Prophet's family), and *awliya Allah* (saints). People are coming to receive those lights.

Madina is the House of Allah *(AJ)*

What do you think then about the lights of *Madinatul munawera*? Now we look at the other part of that hadith.

Baytullah Qalbil mumin (House of Allah is the Heart of the believer)

Qalbil mumin baytullah (Heart of the believer is the House of Allah)

When do you go to Madina? What is in Madina? Prophet (ﷺ). What is there? The *qalbil of the mumin*. The real *qalb* (heart) that Allah *(AJ)* has created. That house (*ka'bah*) *baytul 'atiq* بيت العتيق (the ancient house), is brick and stones that you made with your hands. Allah *(AJ)* made it to be holy by the souls of very holy souls. As a result of their souls and their worship, Allah *(AJ)* wants you to come and be dressed by that light. Like the sun they are emanating lights. You are just imitating, these lights will be dressing you and blessing you. Just like the *imam*, when it comes time to pray; Prophet (ﷺ) is the *Imam*. Prophet's (ﷺ) prayer to Allah *(AJ)* counts and we are the *jama'a* (people following the *Imam* in prayer) in Mecca. But, that is *baytullah qalbil mumin*. *Qalbil mumin* (the heart of the believers) are there.

But, if you go to Madina, this is where the *Mu'min* resides. So what is there? *Baytullah* (house of God). Do we get it? *Baytullah*. When you go to *Madina tul munawera*, Prophet (ﷺ) is in *fana* (annihilation).

Mecca in binary code is one and Madina is zero, *Nuqt*. Prophet (ﷺ) is in complete annihilation. **As a result of annihilation, the heart of the Prophet (ﷺ) is where Allah *(AJ)* is residing;** therefore the light of Allah *(AJ)*, the realities and the divinely presence.

If we don't understand the reality and the relationship of *La ilaha ilAllah, Muhammadun Rasul Allah*, then we are constantly off of our understanding. That's why Prophet (ﷺ) came and brought us and taught us to say *La ilaha ilAllah, La ilaha ilAllah, La ilaha ilAllah*. Make *dhikr* of Allah, Allah, Allah. But what did Allah *(AJ)* teach you to make dhikr of?

In Allaha wa Malayikatahu yusalona alan Nabi.

إِنَّ اللَّهَ وَمَلَائِكَتَهُ يُصَلُّونَ عَلَى النَّبِيِّ يَا أَيُّهَا الَّذِينَ آمَنُوا صَلُّوا عَلَيْهِ وَسَلِّمُوا تَسْلِيماً

33:56 – *Innallaha wa malaaikatahu yusalluna 'alan Nabiyi yaa ayyuhal ladhina aamanu sallu 'alayhi wa sallimu taslimaa. (Surat Al Ahzab)*

"Allah and His angels send blessings on the Prophet: O you that believe! Send your blessings on him, and salute him with all respect."
(The Combined Forces 33:56)

This is the relationship. Prophet (ﷺ) teaches, Mecca. Bring yourself to oneness, understand the greatness of the divinely presence. But, even there is the heart of the believers because Allah's *(AJ)* love is residing there. As a result of Mecca and the acceptance of the *tawaf* of Mecca, Allah *(AJ)* says, now I want you to be dressed by My divinely presence; you go to Madina. *In Allaha wa Malayikatahu yusalona alan Nabi* (Allah and his angels send blessings upon the Prophet (ﷺ)). Forget about the *Ya ayu hal ladhina amano* (oh those who believe). They don't care about the rest. But Allah *(AJ's) dhikr* and *malayika's dhikr* is on *Madina tul Munawera*. Allah's *(AJ) nazar* and presence and divinely lights are in *Madina tul Munawera*. And all *malayika* from the beginning of creation to the end of creation must be present and making *salawat* on Sayyidina Muhammad (ﷺ).

Subhana rabbika rabil 'izzati 'ama yasifoon, Wa salamun 'alal mursaleen wal hamdulillahi rabbil 'alameen. Bi hurmati Muhammadil Mustafa wa bi siratil suratil Fatiha.

THE SECRETS OF THE 12TH MONTH OF THE ISLAMIC LUNAR CALENDAR DHUL HIJJA ذُالْحِجَّة

The Month of Hajj (Pilgrimage) and Sacrifice
The Youthful Innocence and To Be Rabbaniyun

Realities of Prophet Ismail *(as)*, Prophet Yusuf (Joseph) *(as)*, 12th Chapter of Holy Quran is Surah Yusuf and the Realities of the Kawthar

Dhul Hijjah ذُوالْحِجَّة, The Month of Hajj and Pilgrimage

Spiritual Importance of the Moon's Phases

One of the secrets of the lunar calendar that enlightened masters have understood is regarding the moon and the spiritual importance of the moon's phases. The Islamic calendar is based upon the 12 phases of the moon, and each of these 12 phases represents 12 veils, or 12 different emanations that are dressing creation throughout the year.

Imam Ali *(as)* says, "The Prophet was once asked about the Imams while I was in his presence. He answered: I swear by the sky, [displaying] the Zodiacal signs (a reference to 85:1). Their number is the same number of the signs of the Zodiac. I swear by the Lord of the nights, days, and months their number is the same as the number of the months. The companion said: Who are they O messenger of Allah? So the Prophet (ﷺ) placed his hand on my head and said: The first of them is this (Imam Ali) and the last (12th) of them is Al-Mahdi. Whoever supports them has supported me, who ever opposes them opposes me, whoever loves them loves me, whoever disdains them has disdained me, whoever rejects them has rejected me, and whoever acknowledges them has acknowledged me. Through them Allah protects His religion, expands His lands, sustains His people, brings down the drops of the sky, and the blessings of the earth emerge. They are my trustees and successors and the leaders and masters of the believers."

Allah's *(AJ)* Holy Speech Known as Quran is Dressing These Holy Months

At the Level of Sainthood, These *Surahs* Dressing the 12 Months

1.	Al-Fatihah (The opener)	dressing	1.	Muharram مُحَرَّم
2.	Al-Baqarah (The Cow)	dressing	2	Safar صَفَر
3.	'Ali 'Imran (Family of Imran)	dressing	3.	Rabi al Awwal رَبِيعُ الأَوَّلُ (Rabi I)
4.	An-Nisa' (The Women)	dressing	4.	Rabi al Thani رَبِيعُ الثَّانِي
5.	Al-Ma'idah (The Table Spread)	dressing	5.	Jumaada al Olā جَمَادَى الْأُولَي
6.	Al-An'am (The Cattle)	dressing	6.	Jumada alThani جَمَادِ الثَّانِي
7.	Al-A'raf (The Heights)	dressing	7.	Rajab رَجَبْ
8.	Al-Anfal (The Spoils of War)	dressing	8.	Sha'bān شَعْبَانْ
9.	At-Tawbah (The Repentance)	dressing	9.	Ramaḍān رَمَضَانْ
10.	Yunus (Prophet Jonah)	dressing	10.	Shawwāl شَوَّالْ
11.	Hud	dressing	11.	Dhul Qi'da ذُوالْقِعْدَةْ
12.	Yusuf (Prophet Joseph)	dressing	12.	Dhul Hijja ذُوالْحِجَّهْ

In this 12th month we are completing one year of *ma'refah* (gnosticism), one year of spiritual journeying. It is the month of pilgrimage in Sufi tradition, in remembrance of the Prophet Abraham *(as)*. According to Sufi teaching we are all pilgrims, we are all seekers, regardless of whether or not we are making the physical pilgrimage. Our Masters are teaching us that every moment is a pilgrimage for the soul. In every moment and with every passing day we are looking to make a pilgrimage towards perfected character. We are asking to leave bad character and move towards good character and good actions. Then, as we go deeper into the esoteric knowledge of Naqshbandia, these numbers begin to unlock certain secrets which pertain to our individual spiritual development.

For example, each of the 12 months is dressed from the secrets of the corresponding *Surah* (chapter) of the Holy Qur'an. In this 12th month of *Dhul Hijjah*, the secrets of the 12th *Surah*, *Surah Yusuf* (Prophet Joseph (*as*)), begin to dress us, as well as the secrets of the 108th *Surah*, *Surah Kawthar*.

Awliya and Power of Number 9 – The Sultan (King) of Numbers

9 is the Sultan of numbers. Why? Surah 108 is because as we moved from 1 through 9, with 9 being the highest and most powerful number. Saints are moving with the power of 9 in every moment. They have reached to that authority, to that perfection and that power which is symbolized by the number 9. As we enter the 12th month, the month of *Dhul Hijjah*, we are dressed with the secrets of the 12th *Surah*, *Surah Yusuf*.

But the saints are being dressed with the secrets of the 108th *Surah Kawthar* because $9 \times 12 = 108$.

Holy Quran, Surat Al 'Isra (Night Journey) (17:79–81)

وَمِنَ اللَّيْلِ فَتَهَجَّدْ بِهِ نَافِلَةً لَّكَ عَسَىٰ أَن يَبْعَثَكَ رَبُّكَ مَقَامًا مَّحْمُودًا (٧٩)

وَقُل رَّبِّ أَدْخِلْنِي مُدْخَلَ صِدْقٍ وَأَخْرِجْنِي مُخْرَجَ صِدْقٍ وَاجْعَل لِّي مِن لَّدُنكَ سُلْطَانًا نَّصِيرًا (٨٠)

وَقُلْ جَاءَ الْحَقُّ وَزَهَقَ الْبَاطِلُ ۚ إِنَّ الْبَاطِلَ كَانَ زَهُوقًا (٨١)

Wa minal layli fatahajjad bihi nafilatal laka 'asaa an yab'athaka rabbuka maqaman Mahmoda. (79)

Wa qur rabbi adkhilnee mudkhala sidqin wa akhrijneemukhraja sidqin waj'al lee milladunka sultanan naseera (80)

Wa qul jaa al haqqu wa zahaqal batilu, innal batila kaana zahooqa (81)

"And pray in the small watches of the morning: (it would be) an additional prayer (or spiritual profit) for thee: soon will thy Lord raise thee to a Station of Praise and Glory!" (79)

Say: "O my Lord! Let my entry be by the Gate of Truth and Honour, and likewise my exit by the Gate of Truth and Honour; and grant me from Thy Presence an authority to aid (me)." (80)

And say: "Truth has (now) arrived, and Falsehood perished: for Falsehood is (by its nature) bound to perish." (81)

Saints' gnosticism is always based on the power of 9 because 9 represents perfection. Anything after 9 becomes two digits comprised of numbers from 1-9. One of the secrets of 9 is that **9 multiplied by any number will always break down back to 9.** That is why it (9) is the sultan of numbers.

Therefore, in the 1st month we are being dressed with the 1st *Surah Fatiha* but, Saints are taking from the *Fatiha* and **Opening secrets of the 9th *Surah Tawba* (Repentance).** In the 2nd month, they are taking from the 18th *Surah*, and so on. So while we are being dressed in this month by the 12th *Surah*, enlightened masters who have reached to that *sultanat* (Kingdom) are being dressed by the 108th *Surah*.

At the Level of Sainthood, These *Surahs* Dressing the 12 Months

9.	At-Tawbah (The Repentance)	dressing	1.	Muharram مُحَرَّم
18.	Al-Kahf (The Cave)	dressing	2	Safar صَفَر
27.	An-Naml (The Ant)	dressing	3.	Rabi al Awwal رَبِيْعُ الْأَوَّلُ (Rabi I)
36.	Ya-Sin (Ya Seen)	dressing	4.	Rabi al Thani رَبِيْعُ الثَّانِي
45.	Al-Jathiyah (The Crouching)	dressing	5.	Jumaada al Olā جَمَادَى الْأُولَي
54.	Al-Qamar (The Moon)	dressing	6.	Jumada alThani جَمَادِىَالثَّانِي
63.	Al-Munafiqun (The Hypocrites)	dressing	7.	Rajab رَجَبْ
72.	Al-Jinn (The Jinn)	dressing	8.	Sha'bān شَعْبَانْ
81.	At-Takwir (The Overthrowing)	dressing	9.	Ramaḍān رَمَضَانْ
90.	Al-Balad (The City)	dressing	10.	Shawwāl شَوَّالْ
99.	Az-Zalzalah (The Earthquake)	dressing	11.	Dhul Qi'da ذُوالْقِعْدَةُ
108.	Al-Kawthar (The Abundance)	dressing	12.	Dhul Hijja ذُوالْحِجَّهْ

Therefore, in this 12th month, a month in which millions of people are making their pilgrimage and following in the footsteps of the Prophet Abraham – or Sayyidina Ibrahim *(as)* in Arabic – it is important to reflect on his life and his story. This Reality is based on theHoly Quran.

Secrets of *Surat al Kawthar* (The Fountain of Abundance), Holy Quran 108

إِنَّا أَعْطَيْنَاكَ الْكَوْثَرَ (١) فَصَلِّ لِرَبِّكَ وَانْحَرْ (٢) إِنَّ شَانِئَكَ هُوَ الْأَبْتَرُ (٣)

Inna 'atayna kal kawthar (108:1)

Fasali li rabbika wanhar (108:2)

Inna shani-aka huwal abtar. (108:3)

Mawlana Shaykh As-Sayed Nurjan Mirahmadi

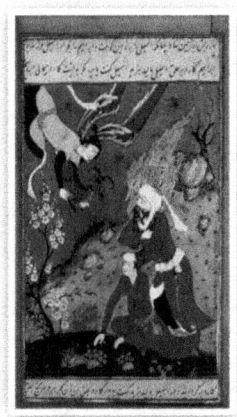

"To thee (O Muhammad) we have granted the Fount (of Abundance). (108:1)

So pray to your Lord and Sacrifice. (108:2)

Indeed, your enemy is the one cut off." (108:3)

Every Prophet and every Messenger of the Divine was sent to humanity as an example for us. Not only did they dedicate their entire lives in service to the Creator, but they were actually created for no other purpose than to teach us about the Divine and how to approach the Divine Presence. If not for their lives and the stories of their lives, we would have no coordinates; we would have no means to approach. It would be like trying to find your way out of a wilderness without a road. This material world is a wilderness and we are lost in its vastness. Things are happening in our lives from left to right and we most likely have no idea why they're happening. Then we open up a Holy Book, any Holy Book, and we read about the lives of the Prophets and we find that they have already blazed a trail for us to follow to quickly get out of this jungle and avoid its dangers. These books and these stories contain tremendous sources of wisdom which help us to navigate this life.

Prophet Ibrahim *(as)* Was Ordered to Sacrifice His Son

As Sufis, we read about the story of Prophet Abraham *(as)* and we contemplate about his life. Prophet Abraham *(as)* was *Khalilulllah*, the "intimate friend of God", and he was known for his amazing generosity.

Anything that his Lord had given to him he gave back to his community. But, from all the blessings that he had enjoyed in his life there remained one thing that he had not been granted. All his life, Sayyidina Ibrahim *(as)* had prayed to his Lord for a son, that would inherit his spirituality, until finally his prayer was answered and Sayidena Ismail *(as)* was born.

$$\text{فَصَلِّ لِرَبِّكَ وَانْحَرْ (٢)}$$

108:2 – Fasali li rabbika wanhar (Surat Al Kawthar)

"So pray to your Lord and Sacrifice." (The Abundance 108:2)

Then an order came to Sayyidina Ibrahim *(as)* that shook his heart. He was ordered to sacrifice his only son Sayyidina Ismail *(as)*. In the morning he is crying, his heart is breaking, and he wakes up his son and says, "babba, we have to go for a walk." And Sayyidina Ismail *(as)* is looking at his father innocently and asking, "what's wrong father?" And Sayyidina Ibrahim *(as)* is not able to answer, but is just trying to maintain his composure and not scare his son. He is trying his best to keep Sayyidina Ismail *(as)* unaware of what is going to happen. At this point in the story, Saints are taking from Heavenly Knowledge, from hidden Knowledge, and are able to explain to us their dialogue that day.

As Sayyidina Ibrahim *(as)* held his son's hand and walked up that mountain, preparing to sacrifice him, his heart was in agony, tears were streaming down his cheeks, but his soul was in submission. Then something miraculous occurred; his son looked at him and said: "Father, why are you crying? I know what you have been asked to do. Tie my hands and God willing, you will find me to be peaceful."

فَلَمَّا بَلَغَ مَعَهُ ٱلسَّعْىَ قَالَ يَٰبُنَىَّ إِنِّىٓ أَرَىٰ فِى ٱلْمَنَامِ أَنِّىٓ أَذْبَحُكَ فَٱنظُرْ مَاذَا تَرَىٰ ۚ قَالَ يَٰٓأَبَتِ ٱفْعَلْ مَا تُؤْمَرُ ۖ سَتَجِدُنِىٓ إِن شَآءَ ٱللَّهُ مِنَ ٱلصَّٰبِرِينَ

37:102 – Falamma balagha ma'ahus sa'ya qala ya bunayya inni ara fee almanami annee adhbahuka fanzhur ma dha tara, Qala ya abati if'al ma tu maru, satajidunee inshaAllahu minas Sabireen. (Surat as Saffat)

"And when he reached with him [the age of] exertion, he said, "O my son, indeed I have seen in a dream that I [must] sacrifice you, so see what you think." He said, "O my father, do as you are commanded. You will find me, if Allah wills, one of the Patient/ steadfast." (Those Who Set the Ranks 37:102)

Mawlana Shaykh is teaching us that there is tremendous wisdom in this story. All his life Prophet Abraham *(as)* gave to his community. The one thing that he wanted all his life was the one thing that the Divine asked him to give up. Divine was teaching us, and Prophet Abraham *(as)* was teaching us through the example of his life, that anyone can give things that they aren't attached to. Some people aren't attached to their money, and they are very generous with it. That is a good characteristic to have, if that money is used in the way of the Divine. However, what is more loved from the Divine is when we are willing to sacrifice those things we want, those things that we struggle to part with.

Can You Sacrifice Your Bad Character For the Sake of Allah *(AJ)*?

It means, are you willing to sacrifice your bad character for the sake of your Creator? Would you stop smoking? Stop gossiping? Stop getting angry? Would you leave your bad character and begin your pilgrimage towards the Heavenly Kingdom? Either way, you are on a pilgrimage to that world because this life is ending, and spiritual teachers are asking us, "What have you done to prepare for that meeting with your Lord?"

فَصَلِّ لِرَبِّكَ وَانْحَرْ (٢)

108:2 – Fasali li rabbika wanhar (Surat Al Kawthar)

"So pray to your Lord and Sacrifice." (The Abundance 108:2)

In the end, Sayyidina Ibrahim *(as)* didn't sacrifice his son, Sayyidina Ismail *(as)* – a ram was given in his place. The Divine is saying, "I didn't need the boy, just like I don't need your prayers or your fasting. O Sayyidina Ibrahim! I don't need anything from you, but I wanted to test the condition of your heart. I wanted to see if you would be willing to sacrifice your ego's desires out of love for Me."

The level of sacrifice that we read in this story is only for Prophets. That is why his story is so powerful, and it is so important to remember his sacrifice at this time of year. It's something we could never imagine having to go through, but always their stories contain wisdoms and lessons for us. Mawlana Shaykh is asking, "Are you willing to sacrifice? Are you willing to leave your desires for the sake of the Divine?" because that is a display of true love.

People can say whatever they like, but it's the actions that count. Prophet (ﷺ) was teaching (from Quran) that on the Day of Judgement your mouth will be sealed and your hands and feet will testify for you.

الْيَوْمَ نَخْتِمُ عَلَىٰ أَفْوَاهِهِمْ وَتُكَلِّمُنَا أَيْدِيهِمْ وَتَشْهَدُ أَرْجُلُهُم بِمَا كَانُوا يَكْسِبُونَ (٦٥)

36:65 – Al yawma nakhtimu 'ala afwahehim wa tukallimunaa aydeehim wa tashhadu arjuluhum bima kanoo yaksiboon. (Surat al Yaseen)

"That Day, We will seal over their mouths, and their hands will speak to Us, and their feet will testify about what they used to earn." (Yasin 36:65)

Why? Because the mouth says many useless things, but what you do with your hands and feet is where the real truth lies. As they say in English, "actions speak louder than words."

Whose Station is Higher – Ibrahim *(as)* or Ismail *(as)*?

There is another secret in the story of Sayyidina Ibrahim *(as)* which is from the knowledge of the *'arifeen*, the "knowers of God." From their knowledge they relate to us a dialogue which occurred between Sayyidina Ibrahim *(as)* and Sayyidina Ismail *(as)*. It is as follows; following his ordeal, Sayyidina Ibrahim *(as)* said to his Lord, "O my Lord! My heart was bleeding and my hands were shaking. I loved my son so much but I heard Your order and I obeyed!" سَمِعْنَا وَأَطَعْنَا *Samina wa 'atana.*

سَمِعْنَا وَأَطَعْنَا غُفْرَانَكَ رَبَّنَا وَاِلَيْكَ الْمَصِيْرُ

2:285 – ...Sam'ina wa ata'na, ghufranaka Rabbana wa ilaykal masir. (Surat al Baqarah)

"*...We hear, and we obey: (We seek) Thy forgiveness, our Lord, and to Thee is the end of all journeys." (Holy Quran, 2:285)*

"It is a testament to my sincerity and my love for You, my Lord!" Sayyidina Ibrahim *(as)* was proud of his level of sacrifice, but Mawlana Shaykh is teaching that if you think Sayyidina Ibrahim *(as)* reached a high station of spiritual submission, what about the boy?!

فَصَلِّ لِرَبِّكَ وَانْحَرْ (٢)

108:2 – Fasali li rabbika wanhar (Surat Al Kawthar)

"*So pray to your Lord and Sacrifice." (The Abundance 108:2)*

Sayyidina Ismail *(as)* was also a Prophet of God. He knew what was happening when his father was leading him up that hill – and he didn't object! He had the faith of what we call in Arabic, a *RijjalAllah* (man of God), combined with the innocence of youth. That combination is the perfection of character that we are seeking in Sufism; to have that type of faith while maintaining a youthful innocence. Children are innocent; they have no plots, no ill plans or conspiracies, but we don't understand that because we're sick and we think everyone else is sick like us.

Secret Realities of Hajj

From the knowledge of Saints they are teaching us that there was a dialogue, and Sayyidina Ismail *(as)* was asking: "O my father, who is higher, you or me?" Sayyidina Ibrahim *(as)* answered, *"O my son, I am higher. You can't imagine how difficult it was to be asked to give up the one thing you wanted your entire life, to be asked to sacrifice something you love so dearly."* Sayyidina Ismail *(as)* replies, *"No father, I am higher, for you were merely sacrificing your property, while I was accepting to sacrifice myself!"* No one enjoys having to sacrifice anything – so imagine sacrificing yourself, imagine giving your own physicality to be slaughtered and to submit and be at peace with it. Divine is saying, "That level is unimaginable!" And that reality of Sayyidina Ismail *(as)* is being inherited by Sayyidina Muhammad (ﷺ), and all of the *Ahul Bayt*, because Prophet (ﷺ) is the descendant of Sayyidina Ismail *(as)* and He (ﷺ) is the owner of the *Kawthar*.

Secret of Surat al Kawthar

108th Surah (12×9=108), *Surat al Kawthar*

So as we are remembering the sacrifice of Prophet Abraham *(as)* in this 12th month of *Dhul Hijjah*, then Saints begin to teach us from their *Ma'rifat*, from their level of knowledge, which opens a reality from the *Surah al Kawthar*. A s*urah* which is dressing this (12th) holy month of sacrifice when Allah *(AJ)* says:

فَصَلِّ لِرَبِّكَ وَانْحَرْ (٢)

108:2 – *Fasali li rabbika wanhar (Surat al Kawthar)*

"So pray to your Lord and Sacrifice." (The Abundance 108:2)

From their spiritual station and their mystical knowledge, Mawlana Shaykh is teaching that these two oceans are meeting and unlocking their secrets in this month – the story of Sayyidina Ismail *(as)* and Sayyidina Ibrahim *(as)*, and the 108th *Surah* of Holy Qur'an, *(Surah al Kawthar)*.

From the secrets of the story of Sayyidina Ismail *(as)* which is dressing *Dhul Hijjah*, it means "sacrifice yourself!" And God is confirming that reality, saying, *Fa-salli li-Rabbika wanhar*, "pray unto thy Lord and sacrifice" (108:2). It means that as long as you take care of yourself, you will achieve nothing, but if you sacrifice from what is most dear to you, if you sacrifice from your own physicality, Divine says "I will take care of you." Put yourself on that block; sacrifice your bad character and bad habits. Place no importance on the physicality by allowing your body to experience pain and discomfort; and ask the Divine for support in moving towards good character and for support in making the real pilgrimage of the self in this holy month.

إِنَّ شَانِئَكَ هُوَ الْأَبْتَرُ (٣)

108:3 – Inna shani-aka huwal abtar. (Surat al Kawthar)

"Indeed, your enemy is the one cut off." (The Abundance 108:3)

Only Allah *(AJ)* can cut our enemies off the biggest enemy is the ego and *Shaytan*. Then, the miracle of the Divine is that if you sacrifice, the Divine will take care of you. But first you must be saying "O my Lord! Thy will be done! I don't need my will." You can say it by tongue, but there must also be an action. If that prayer enters into your heart, and you are really submitting your will to Divine's will, God says "I will give you the treasures of Heaven and earth."

Subhana rabbika rabil 'izzati 'ama yasifoon, Wa salamun 'alal mursaleen wal hamdulillahi rabbil 'alameen. Bi hurmati Muhammadil Mustafa wa bi siratil suratil Fatiha.

REALITIES OF THE CIRCLE AND SECRETS OF HAJJ

In the beginning there was a dot: all the power of the Quran is in *Surat al-Fatiha*, and all the power of *Fatiha* is in *Bismillahir Rahmanir Raheem*, and all the power of *Bismillahir Rahmanir Raheem* is in the *bah*, and all the power of the *bah* ب is in the *nuqt* (Dot).

- Divine Oneness – Wanting to be known
- Circumference – is **Shariah** or Laws of Nature
- Radius – **Tariqah** of way to Divine
- Each Step- on the Radius is **Marifah** – Knowledge of the Divine Truth or Haqq
- **Haqiqah** or Knowledge of the Truth – is the approach to the Divine Center
- **Azimah** – Is Might and Greatness of The Center or Nucleus of Creation

Secret Realities of Hajj

Our First Hajj Was in the Womb

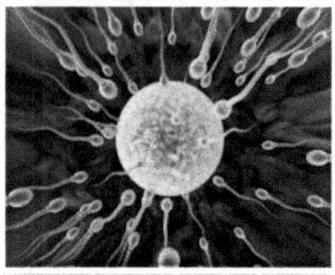

The expansion of creation is symbolized by the border of the circle, the circumference. The *Surat al-Fatiha* is symbolized by circles and the Divine kingdom is within.

Outside is the Divine essence which supports creation.

At the center, The Divine said, "I was a hidden treasure wanting to be known."

كُنْتُ كَنْزاً مخفِيا فَأَحْبَبْتُ أَنْ أُعْرَفَ؛ فَخَلَقْتُ خَلْقاً فَعَرَّفْتهمْ بِي فَعَرَفُونِي

Kuntu kanzan makhfiyya, fa ahbabtu an a'rafa, fa khalaqtu khalqan, fa 'arraftahum bi fa 'arafonee.

"I was a hidden Treasure then I desired to be known, so I created a creation to which I made Myself known; then they knew Me."

The center wants to be known, so direct yourself to the Divine kingdom; seek to find the way to the center!

The Divine is the center needing to be known and Creation, all the points on the circumference, is in need of The Divine as it is the center of Power. In this relationship, based on love, Allah *(AJ)* wants to be known and wants us to be loved. Don't be lost in what people define as "religion" as you seek the path to the center.

The line from the center to the perimeter is the radius. Each radius is a Messenger, a Prophet, those with whom Allah *(AJ)* is satisfied "Radi". They are the Pillars of Creation; they hold the circle together, for without them there can be no circle. They deliver the message – "This is your Creator, this is who you are to worship, and you must follow this discipline in order to reach the center." An atom with a nucleus as its center of power.

Each radius also leads *back* into the center; and the *Nabis* (Prophets) are the big pillars. We are taking the main radius of Prophet Muhammad (ﷺ) and within that are the "inner ways", the *tariqats*. The circle is *Shariah* and everything to do with the circle is the law, and you cannot go outside it.

Tariqat – As soon as you say "I want to take the way", then you are on that way. You have joined the people of *Marifah*, on the way to knowledge of the center, Gnosticism.

Haqiqat – Every step you take on the way is truth, *Haqiqat*. When you reach the center you gain Divine Knowledge of the center, which opens *Haqaiq* (realities) for you. Then you have knowledge of the entire circle because you hold all the spokes that reach the circumference.

In this Allah *(AJ)* shows you that you cannot be outside the circle because from the physical level to the atomic level you are in an ocean of atoms. Your smallest level is your atom and it submits better than your physicality. Within its nucleus all the electrons are circumambulating. THAT is the circle of life and there is no escaping it.

The fastest path to the center is the one with most power and the knowledge of living saints. The Naqshbandi way takes you to the center by way of living connected saints who are full of power. That is why Naqshbandi associations are alive. When we begin, with authorization, to do *dhikr*, they have authority from the Saint of Light to re-synch hearts that are disconnected from universal beat. This is the Hajj.

Hajj is to submit to that reality; we must once in our lifetime open ourselves to that understanding. At Hajj everyone puts on the dress of white – of light – which shows that they are equal in the eyes of Allah *(AJ)* regardless of their education, economic status or skin color.

Al Harmain Mecca – Place of No Forbidden, "The Heart"

Come to the Holy Precincts – the *Ka'bah*, with *Safa* and *Marwa*; the *Ka'bah* is *mim*. The *Ka'bah* represents the nucleus of your existence; you circumambulate and praise your Lord for your existence in the same way the planets circle the sun/Light and the electrons whirl around the nucleus of the atom. As soon as pilgrims begin *tawaf*, all individual differences are put aside and the scattered bits of light come together as an Ocean of Oneness, *Wahdaniyyah*.

Make *tawaf*, circumambulate around the *Ahadiyyah*, the unique Oneness center, and know that you have approached the unique station of the *Kabah*.

Mawlana shows us how that is happening every moment of our lives.

The Hajj or Pilgrimage of Life
The First Hajj Is In the Womb

Allah *(AJ)* / The Divine shows us, in the womb of the mother is the same circle, where the Hajj takes place on a microscopic scale. The *Ahadiyyah* / Unique Oneness is The Egg and the 500,000 sperm (named *mani* in Arabic) are *hajjis*, all vying with each other to reach it in order to be *Abdullah* / Servant of God. The one that reaches the egg will get to the station of creation; that <u>one seed</u> will go into the *Ka'bah* of the womb, do its *khalwah* (isolation) for nine months and come out as a new creation.

You Had the Winning Gift

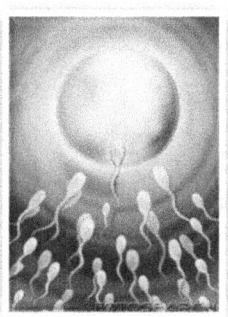

From The Divine one survived while the other 499,999 did not; you were the miracle and are already blessed and loved by the Divine. Mawlana says to you, now do this a second time, I am bringing you to *marifah* of the soul.

So take your body and make *tawaf* and ask Allah *(AJ)* "*Ya Rabbi*/O My Lord, it is not enough to be on the outside. Let me go inside the *Ka'bah*."

This time Allah *(AJ)* says, "Yes you can, this *Ka'bah* represents the heart of Sayyidina Muhammad (ﷺ), just as your soul came from *mani*, Muhammadan Nur."

All prophets are brothers in the brotherhood of the Prophet (ﷺ), and whatever prophet you love is the reality you are seeking. Everyone around the circle has the same center. Allah *(AJ)* is saying jump into that center, jump into the *Ka'bah*, the Prophetic station, the lights of *marifah* (Gnostics).

Don't keep thinking it is Hajj and everybody is going to visit Saudi Arabia. It is more than that. Now Mawlana is asking you to be more specific in your request. "*Ya Rabbi*, let me go to the heart of Prophet (ﷺ), open the doors of Prophet's (ﷺ) heart." If you are in this association you have been granted permission to ask that because your soul is from Naqshbandi realities. We are asking to open the door of Sayyidina Muhammad's (ﷺ) heart.

All you see during *dhikr* is *Ka'ba Sharif* and you are asking Prophet Muhammad (ﷺ) to let you go into his heart, to make *tawaf* there with the soul of *Sultan al-Awliya* and the soul of Mawlana Shaykh Al Qabbani. A high reality was reached by those who came here to visit their Shaykhs.

The Shaykhs Are the Living Kabah and the Qibla

Furthermore, the one who goes to Cyprus is a real *Hajji*; that is a gift for the seeker. One destination is obvious – visited by 3 million people, but only 300 people visited the secret destination. That is a secret in the night sky – the tiny stars can show you the way. But during the day there is no guidance like that.

You turned to the living *Qibla* and came to the living *Kabah*. This is Mawlana Shaykh; he is in the presence of Sayyidina Muhammad (ﷺ). As we make way around our Shaykh with our praise and our love, we are in the presence of Muhammadan reality. When we pray to Allah *(AJ)* and know that Mawlana is our *Imam* in his direction, it is as if we are praying in the Divine Presence, praying in the presence of Prophet Muhammad (ﷺ) to Allah *(AJ)*.

Which then is holier, *Ka'bah* or That which Allah *(AJ)* made with His Two Hands? If you think bricks and stones are holier, which are made from Men, then that is idol worshipping. It is the presence of Sayyidina Muhammad (ﷺ), *Rabb al-Bayt*, which is what makes the *Ka'bah* holy. Then if Prophet's (ﷺ) emanation is on *Bani Adam* whom Allah *(AJ)* created with His Two Hands, then the Shaykhs' secret is much higher.

When we accept the guides in our heart, he is the *Kabah*. Shaykh al Hisham is the reflection of Shaykh Nazim al Haqqani, Sultan al-Awliya, and when we dress ourselves in the Shaykh we invite that *Ka'bah* (Shaykh Nazim) into our lives. When you believe and understand that he is *everything* in your life, then Prophet (ﷺ) opens the City of Lights. *Medina Munawira*.

Then we need to get into the *Ka'bah*. Once you get into the *Ka'bah*, there is a secret highway underground to the city of the Prophet (ﷺ). Visualize that you are going into the Prophetic (ﷺ) heart, and ask "Dress me  from Mawlana Shaykh and let me go to the City of Lights, *Madina al-Munawira*." Now He brings His light. That is what we are aspiring to — these are days of *marifah*.

Arafat is the station of knowing. We went to the *Ka'bah* and laid ourselves to be sacrificed like a lamb; let us be *halal* for Sayyidina Muhammad (ﷺ). Let us each say "*Ya Rabbi*, my head is on the floor, I don't know anything nor should I claim to know anything until I have tasted from that reality. Let the *Zabiha* (sacrifice) take place and take away "what I think of myself" and "what I don't know."

Subhana rabbika rabil 'izzati 'ama yasifoon, Wa salamun 'alal mursaleen wal hamdulillahi rabbil 'alameen. Bi hurmati Muhammadil Mustafa wa bi siratil suratil Fatiha.

REALITY OF HAJJ

Your 7 Names in 7 Paradises, 7 Tawaf

Four Groups
Nabiyeen (Prophets), Siddiqeen (Truthful), Shuhada (Witness), wa Saleheen (Righteous)

Always an advice and reminder for myself that *alhamdulillah* we are in the nights of *Eid ul Adha* and for *Ahlul Muhabbat*, and the lovers of Sayyidina Muhammad (ﷺ) they put their entire support upon the love of Prophet (ﷺ).

To know with all your heart, and all your belief, that, *Yaa Rabbi*, I am going to come short in every *'amal*, in every action. And I am not going to reach Your satisfaction, as those who came before us, in the level of their piety, in the level of their sincerity, and in the level of their accomplishments. *Yaa Rabbi* we put our hopes on the love of Sayyidina Muhammad (ﷺ).

What Allah *(AJ)* (Mighty and Majestic) is dressing Sayyidina Muhammad (ﷺ) and all the prophets with, then with no doubt to know that Prophet (ﷺ) is dressing us. That in this *dunya*, which is not even the weight of a mosquito for the Divinely Presence and anyone who loves the Divinely Presence. How much Prophet (ﷺ) cared for his Nation in *dunya*, imagine the love that Prophet (ﷺ) has for us in *Akhirah*? That, *yaa Rabbi*, "whatever You are granting to me, it doesn't have its flavour if I don't dress my Nation and I don't give them those dressings, and especially the *Ahlul Muhabbat* (people of love), who are trying to be the first in line.

2:269 – *Yutee al hikmata man yashao wa man yuta al hikmata faqad ootiya khayran katheeran wa ma yath thakkaru illa oloo al-albab. (Surat al Baqara)*

"*He granteth wisdom to whom He pleaseth; and he to whom wisdom is granted receiveth indeed a benefit overflowing; but none will grasp the Message but men of understanding/ Men of The Door.*" (Holy Quran 2:269)

Lovers of Prophet (ﷺ) Are the People of the Door

That is why they are called *Ahbaab an Nabi* احباب النبي (Lovers of Prophet (ﷺ) and *Ulul al Baab* أُولِي الألباب "people of the door" and it rhymes with the lovers. The lovers of Sayyidina Muhammad (ﷺ), they are at the door of Prophet (ﷺ).

"انا مدينة العلم و علي بابها"

"ana madinatul-ilmin wa `aliyyun baabuha."

"I am city of knowledge and `Ali is the door."
Prophet Muhammad (ﷺ)

And never anyone coming to the door of Sayyidina Muhammad (ﷺ), *Ashaab an-Nabi* (ﷺ), *Ahl al-Bayt Nabi* (ﷺ), will ever be turned away, will ever be sent away empty handed. Impossible! It is against our belief. It is against everything that the heart knows to be true, that love is something unimaginable. That with that understanding of love, *yaa Rabbi* we are trying so hard to show our love for You.

"Awliyaohu illal Muttaqona"

Who Are the Real Custodians of the Holy House of Allah *(AJ)*

8:34 – Wa ma lahum alla yu'adhdhibahumu Allahu wa hum yasuddona 'anil masjidil harami wa ma kano awliya ahu, in awliyaohu illal Muttaqona wa lakinna aktharahum la ya'lamon. (Surat al Anfal)

"But what plea have they that Allah should not punish them, when they keep out (men) from the sacred Mosque – and <u>they are not its guardians</u>? No men can be its guardians except the High Level Consciousness / Muttaqeen; but most of them do not understand." (The Spoils of War 8:34)

Secret of Holy Ka'bah

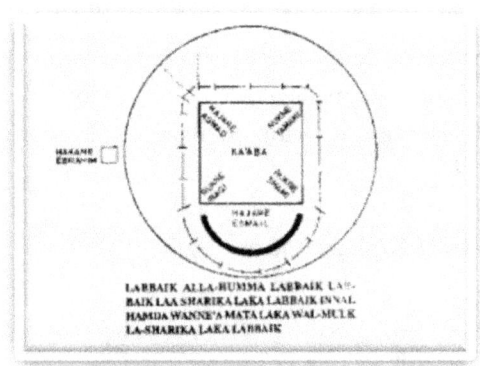

Nabiyyeen, Siddiqeen, Shuhada wa Saliheen

Then they remind of the secret of the Holy *Ka'bah* and why you make *tawaf*? What is the understanding of that *Ka'bah*? That is *tajjaliyaat* of the Holy House of Allah *(AJ)*, but Allah *(AJ)* is not located in that house. Nothing is *shareek* (partner), nothing is *shabee*, nothing is like unto Allah *(AJ)*. Allah *(AJ)* clarifies in Holy Qur'an that Allah *(AJ)* is with the *Nabiyyeen, Siddiqeen, Shuhada wa Saliheen* and our whole life is based on that reality.

4:69 – Wa man yuti' Allaha war Rasola fa olayeka ma'al ladheena an'ama Allahu 'alayhim minan Nabiyeena, was Siddiqee na, wash Shuhadai, was Saliheena wa hasuna olayeka rafeeqan. (Surat an Nisa)

"And whoever obeys Allah and the messenger, then those are with the ones on whom Allah bestowed his Favors amongst the prophets, the highly Righteous [Truthful], the Witnesses to the truth, and the Righteous. And Ah! what a beautiful fellowship!" (The Women 4:69)

Yaa Rabbi, we are coming to Your Holy House. They teach us that what makes that House to be holy, that if they are wanting the Presence of Allah *(AJ)* then the *arwah* (souls) of the *Nabiyyeen* (prophets), 124,000 *Nabiyyeen*, their *arwah*, their souls, must be present.

The soul, they can take a portion of it. We described before, that *malakoot* (heavenly realm) is not the logic of *mulk* (material world). *Mulk* is this cup and this cup is two cups. *Malakoot* is this drop of water with that drop of water is still one drop of water. You can have ten drops of water or ten drops of Light, they are only one Light. Means that Light of *Nabiyyeen* can be wherever Allah *(AJ)* wants them to be.

What Makes Holy Ka'bah to be Holy?

But what is making the Holy *Ka'bah* to be holy are the 124,000 *Nabiyyeen*, 124,000 *Siddiqeen*, 124,000 *Shuhada*, who must be on the Earth anytime. That they [*Shuhada*] are inheriting from the *Siddiqeen*, and the *Siddiqeen* are inheriting from the *Nabiyyeen*. And the door for us is to be with the *Saliheen*.

They (*saliheen*) are teaching us that when you are making that *tawaf* and you are coming to the House, that Allah *(AJ)* sanctified and purified; it is because what is in the House is important. What are in the precincts are the Lights and the souls of 124,000 prophets, *Siddiq's, Shuhada*, those who see, and the *Saliheen*. Means their *arwah* and their Lights are always emanating; and because of what Allah *(AJ)* dressed their Lights, not the stones, not the bricks.

Secret Realities of Hajj

It's funny that those people who run that area and they don't believe in any *tabarruk* (blessing), why do they sell the *Kiswah* (cloth that covers the *Ka'bah*)? If you bring a *tabarruk* and a blessing from *Madina Munawarah* or from anywhere on Earth, they say, "No!" Why then are you selling the *Kiswah* of holy *Ka'bah*? Maybe it makes a lot of money. But there is a tremendous *barakah*. Why? Because the *tajalli* (manifestation) that Allah *(AJ)* is dressing upon that fabric, upon those stones, but it is not directed to them, it is directed to the souls and the Light that is within them, the *arwah* that are within them! That is what makes it to be holy.

9:19 – Aja'altum Siqayatal Hajja Wa 'Imaratal Masjidil Haraami Kaman Amana Billahi, Wal Yawmil Akhiri, Wa Jahada Fi Sabilillahi, La Yastaoona 'Indallahi, Wallahu La Yahdil Qamaz Zalimeen. (Surat At Tawbah)

"Do ye make the giving of drink to pilgrims or the maintenance of the Sacred Mosque, equal to (the pious service of) those who believe in Allah and the Last Day and strive with might and main in the cause of Allah? They are not comparable in the sight of Allah: and Allah doesn't guide those who do wrong." (The Repentance 9:19)

Are You Making Sajdah (Prostration) to Ka'bah?

And that's why when you come across holy people, you describe them as your *Ka'bah* and your *Qibla*. It takes *tafakkur*. Because anyone who is making *sajda*, should be very clear that they are not making *sajda* for the *Ka'bah*. Otherwise you are *'bodt parast'*, you are an idol worshipper. Means you are facing the *Ka'bah*, Prophet (ﷺ) trusted enough that you understood, you are facing this stone house, but you better not be worshiping it. But then they come and they are rubbing themselves all over the stones.

The people of *ma'rifah*, and the people of realities, they understood that they are bowing down to the majesty of the Light that Allah *(AJ)* which is emanating in that location. Not the stones. Not the structure that man built, but the Light that Allah *(AJ)* is sending there. What is noble about that sanctuary that, no *haram*, is the location of the souls that are amination and are continuously circumambulating within that precinct. Allah *(AJ)* grants them that their souls never to leave, and they are in a continuous *tawaf* and the center of energy and the *tajjali* that is dressing.

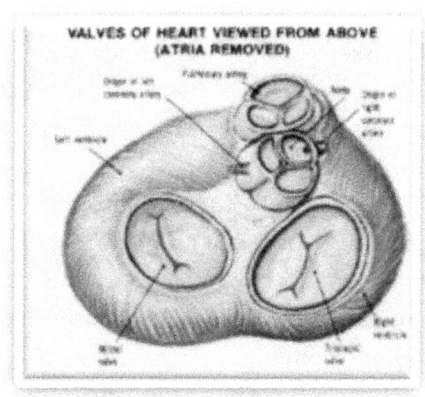

And as a result Allah *(AJ)* made the secrets of Hajj that you have to make seven *tawaf* around that heart, around that Holy *Ka'bah* which is symbolic of the Divinely Heart. Where Allah *(AJ)* says: If you want My Presence come and make *tawaf* but this presence of Mine, you will never find Me, I am a Hidden Treasure wanting to be known through the *Nabiyyeen*, through the *Siddiqeen*, through the *Shuhada* and the *Saliheen*.

Kuntu kanzan makhfiyya, fa ahbabtu an a'rafa, fa khalaqtu khalqan, fa 'arraf tahum bi fa 'arafonee.

"I was a hidden Treasure then I desired to be known, so I created a creation to which I made Myself known; then they knew Me." (Hadith Qudsi)

Holy Associations Must Have of the Saliheen and Shuhada

17.72 – Wa man kana fee hadhihi a'ma fahuwa fee al akhirati a'ma wa adallu sabeela. (Surat al Isra)

"But those who were blind in this world, will be blind in the hereafter, and most astray from the path." (The Night Journey 17:72)

We said many times in our teachings that your association must have of the *Saliheen* if you want to be with Allah *(AJ)*. In any association, you look to the association and is there *Saliheen* amongst them? If there is a *Saliheen*, there must be someone from the *Shuhada*/Witnesses. If they have no *Ahl as-Shuhood* and no *Ahl al-Basira* in their association they are lacking from the *Saliheen*. It means they cannot accomplish to be *Saliheen*, if they don't have somebody who is *Shuhada*/Witnesses, somebody who is not blind in the association. If somebody who is blind is leading the association, everybody will be blind in that association. What didn't work for him or her, won't work for five thousand other people behind them.

So the *Ka'bah* is symbolizing and teaching to us: you want to be with Me, make sure always your life is filled with *Saliheen* who are connected to the *Shuhada*/ Witnesses. And those *Shuhada* they are very connected to the *Siddiqeen*. Means they are either coming from Sayyidina Abu Bakr Siddiq *(ra)* or from Sayyidina 'Ali *(as)*. These are the *turuqs*, these are the people of the Path of Realities. And they take from the heart of the *Nabiyyeen*, the greatest and the *imam* of all the prophets, Sayyidina Muhammad (ﷺ). That is unbroken, *ati ullah, ati ar-rasul wa ulul amri minkum*. Those are all the *ulul amr* in our life.

يَـٰٓأَيُّهَا ٱلَّذِينَ ءَامَنُوٓا۟ أَطِيعُوا۟ ٱللَّهَ وَأَطِيعُوا۟ ٱلرَّسُولَ وَأُو۟لِى ٱلْأَمْرِ مِنكُمْ ...

4:59 – *Ya ayyu hal latheena amanoo Atiu Allaha wa atiur Rasola wa Ulil amre minkum...(Surat an-Nisa)*

"O You who have believed, Obey Allah, obey the Messenger, and those in authority among you." (The Women, 4:59)

Secret of 7 *Tawaf* – 7 Names in 7 Paradises

67:3 – *Alladhee khalaqa sab`a samawatin Tibaqan, ma tara fee khalqir Rahmani min tafawutin farji`e albasara hal tara min futoor. (Surat al Mulk)*

"[And] who created seven heavens in layers. You do not see in the creation of the Most Merciful any inconsistency. So return [your] vision [to the sky]; do you see any breaks?" (Holy Quran 67:3)

Then they describe make your seven *tawaf*, why you make seven *tawaf*? Because you have seven names in seven Paradises. As soon as you make *tawaf*, you must have a name in the presence of the *Saliheen*, and they know you by that name. You must have a name in the presence of the *Shuhada*. There is a name that Allah *(AJ)* granted to you the day you become *shuhood*, that you will be known to them by that name. And you have a name amongst the *Siddiqeen*. That the day that Allah *(AJ)* makes you to be purified and truthful, that you inherit from them and they dress you from their secret, that you have a *siddiqiya* name in their presence. That is why we said the *tawaf* around the *Ka'bah* is not one time tourist event, it's a life-long event. It is the last of the Pillars because we are supposed to know all of its realities, then we make our Hajj.

But, now Hajj is the concept that you do everything bad and at the end when you have saved up money for a nice vacation, you go, you don't really know what you are doing there, and you come home. And you say, "Now I am clean and I can go into the grave." That was not the reality that Prophet (ﷺ) set for us. That without knowing it, you are idol worshiping, bowing down to something you don't understand its reality, circumambulating something you don't understand its purpose.

Ahl ul-Ma'rifah come into our lives and begin to teach us, there is a tremendous symbol and that *tawaf* is a *tawaf* for all our lives. That, *yaa Rabbi*, let me always circumambulate and be in the company of the *Nabiyyeen;* it means my life has to be filled with the love of Prophet (ﷺ). Always from the teachings of the *Siddiqeen*, who are the great big *siddiq's* that brought all the *turuqs* and all the ways of *ma'rifah*, and *haqqaaiq*. That all the *imams* took from them, whether they are the *imams* from *Ahl al-Bayt* or *imams* of *Ahl as-Sunnah*, all of them took from those realities. And who are the great big *Shuhada* and *Ahl al-Basira*, all those *'ulama* (scholars) who wrote these volumes of books. They were not blind leading the blind. And as a result, because of their *firasat*, because of their hearts, what emanates through them dresses everyone in their associations; whether they be near them or far away from them, their soul reaches.

As a result Allah *(AJ)* describes in Holy Qur'an then: you are with Me and I am with you. Means we have to know our name amongst the *Nabiyyeen*. As soon as we know the name amongst the *Nabiyyeen*, then there must be an opening from Prophet (ﷺ) for the *arwah* and the soul that is sincere, will be invited within the *Ka'bah*.

That you kept the company of what Allah *(AJ)* wanted, Allah is with you, you are with Allah *(AJ)*, and Prophet (ﷺ) is facing that Holy Ka'bah.

9:119 – Ya ayyuhal ladheena amanoo ittaqollaha wa kono ma'as sadiqeen. (Surat at Tawba)

"*O you who have believed, fear Allah and be with those who are true.*"
(The Repentance 9:119)

Your Names in the Ocean of Fana and Baqa – Support and Guide You

And there are two doors that open. And each door has a heart on them, because these are the people of love and *muhabbat*. When that door opens, Allah *(AJ)* gives permission for the name that you have in that  presence, five names. You have a name in the ocean of *fana* 6th, which you have annihilated, and you have a name in the ocean of *baqa* 7th, which Allah *(AJ)* raised you in His Divinely Presence. Each of these names will be a support for your life. That your name amongst the

Saliheen is a continuous dress to you, which blesses you, and guides you, and lifts you.

It means if you take a life-long path that I want to know myself. "Who knows himself will know his Lord."

مَنْ عَرَفَ نَفْسَهُ فَقَدْ عَرَفَ رَبَّهُ

Man 'arafa nafsa hu faqad 'arafa Rabba hu.

"Who knows himself, knows his Lord." Prophet Muhammad (ﷺ)

This is what Prophet (ﷺ) was describing. That take a path of knowing your heart, take a path to circumambulate the outside heart, in order for you to learn your inside heart.

Your Names Lift You Up From Saliheen, Shuhada, Siddiqeen, to Nabiyeen

1. If you circumambulate you will know the *Saliheen*, you will know your name amongst the *Saliheen*. You need to know that name for it to dress you and bless you. And it continuously, is like a rope from Allah *(AJ)*, that keeps dressing you and lifting you.

2. Your next name amongst the *Shuhada* inspires you from *Ahl al-Basira* that: don't forget in this Paradise, in this reality that open your heart and witness the reality. Not that you read it or you hear it, but you have to taste the reality.

3. Then the name amongst the *Siddiqeen* is the name that gives the character, the perfection of the struggling, to reach to what they want you to reach of the perfection of character, so that they can present you to the heavenly presence of Sayyidina Muhammad (ﷺ).

Reality of Kissing Hajar ul Aswad

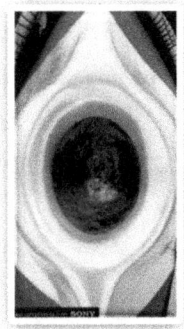

This means *Hajar ul Aswad* is a description and a symbol for us, that if you can reach to the name amongst the *Nabiyyeen*, and reach to that reality, what is the symbol is not from *dunya* any more. It means to kiss the black stone is as if you are kissing the right hand of Sayyidina Muhammad (ﷺ). Why does it look like a ring? It has that silver around it.

The Black Stone
Mecca, Saudi Arabia
Kaaba

That *Yaa Rabbi* let me to reach to You. And Allah *(AJ)* says in Qur'an: you want Me, you can't be *shareek* and think you are reaching My Presence, there is nothing like Me. But you want Me, be with the *Nabiyyeen*.

4:69 – Wa man yuti' Allaha war Rasola faolayeka ma'al ladheena an'ama Allahu 'alayhim minan Nabiyeena, was Siddiqee na, wash Shuhadai, was Saliheena wa hasuna olayeka rafeeqan. (Surat an Nisa)

"And whoever obeys Allah and the messenger, then those are with the ones on whom Allah bestowed his softness amongst the prophets, the highly Righteous [Truthful], the Witnesses to the truth, and the Righteous. And Ah! what a beautiful fellowship!" (The Women 4:69)

As soon as you get to *Hajar ul Aswad, yaa Rasul al-Kareem, yaa Habib al-Azheem*, for God's sake, please take me in, dress me, bless me, grant me my name amongst your presence; a noble name that we came from the oceans of the *Siddiq*. What is a noble name? Only with that noble name can you sit in the presence of Sayyidina Muhammad (ﷺ). That grant me that name, dress me from that name, and allow me an audience and a company in your heavenly presence. So all *mashayikh*

Secret Realities of Hajj

have a Muhammadan name, which includes the name of Sayyidina Muhammad (ﷺ) on that name.

3:31 – *Qul in kuntum tuhibbon Allaha fattabi'onee, yuhbibkumUllahu wa yaghfir lakum dhunobakum wallahu Ghaforur Raheem (Surat Al 'Imran 3:31)*

Say: "If ye do Want Allah love , Be a Follower of me/ Muhammad: Allah will love you and forgive you your sins: For Allah is Oft-Forgiving, Most Merciful." (Family of Imran 3:31)

Ka'bah's Two Doors – Who Are *Ulel Albab* (People of the Door)

If Prophet (ﷺ) grants that opening, what does he grant? An accounting degree? He says, "Come to my heart. You see the two doors? The two ways, either from Abu Bakr Siddiq *(ra)* or from Imam 'Ali *(as)*, come into my heart, because we are with Allah *(AJ)* and Allah *(AJ)* is with us,"

"انا مدينة العلم و علي بابها"

"*ana madinatul-ilmin wa 'aliyyun baabuha.*"

"I am city of knowledge and 'Ali is the door."

79:80 – *wa qul Rabbi adkhelni mudkhala Sidqin wa akhrejni mukhraja Sidqin waj'al li min ladunka Sultanan NaSeera. (Surat al Isra)*

Say: "O my Lord! Let my entry be by the Gate of Truth and Honour, and likewise my exit by the Gate of Truth and Honour; and grant me from Thy Presence an authority [a Sultan] to aid (me)." (The Night Journey 79:80)

39:18 – Alladhina yastame'onal qawla fayattabe'ona aHsanahu, Olaayeka alladhina Hadahumullahu, wa Olaayeka hum Olul Al bab. (Surat Az Zumar)

"Who listen to speech and follow the best of it. Those are the ones Allah has guided, and those are people of understanding. [People of the Door]" (The Troops 39:18)

And the soul enters into that presence and is given a name within that reality and their *arwah* carries a name. At that point Allah *(AJ)* describes: *ayatun min ayatullah*, you are a sign from My Divinely Signs. This is Qur'an. The Arabs have to understand it, not us. If they teach the reality in English. If someone knows Arabic you should go back and read more slower, more careful.

38:29 – Kitabun anzalnahu elayka mubarakun layaddabbaro Ayaatehi wa leyatazakkara Olul Albab. (Surat Swad)

"It is a Book [Quran] We have sent down to you, full of blessing, so let people of intelligence [People of the Door] ponder (liyaddabbaru) its Signs and take heed." (Holy Quran, Saad 38:29)

That Allah *(AJ)* describes that you become the sign of Allah's *(AJ)* Signs and your Light is within that *Ka'bah*, and they begin to call you, that you are like a *Ka'bah*. Not to be worshipped, because you shouldn't be worshipping the *Ka'bah* either. Because they come back and say, "Are you telling people to worship people?" We say No! You shouldn't be worshipping the *Ka'bah*. You worship only Allah *(AJ)*.

Nabbiyeen, Siddiqeen, Shuhada was Saliheen Are Walking Ka'bah

They become walking *Ka'bahs* because the Light is within them emanating from the Divinely Presence. Allah *(AJ)* says: I am with them, that heart is from the *Nabbiyyeen, Siddiqeen, Shuhada was Saliheen*.

Qalb al mu'min baytur rabb.

"The heart of the believer is the House of the Lord."

I am with that heart; that heart now wherever it walks, it is like a *Ka'bah*. It means it gives signs and *isharats*. It gives signs of Allah's *(AJ)* Divinely Presence and love of Sayyidina Muhammad, (ﷺ).

ما وسعني ارضي و لا سمايئ ولاكن وسعني قلب عبدي المؤمن ۞

Maa wasi`anee ardee wa laa samayee wa laakin wasi`anee qalbi `abdee al-mu'min.

"Neither My Earth nor My Heavens can contain Me, but the heart of my Believing Servant." (Hadith Qudsi)

If that heart has that reality it will be dressed like a *Qibla*. *Qibla* means you find your way and your compass to the Divinely Presence, not something to be worshipped. The *Qibla* is something in your life, that when you look at them and look at these pious people, they remind you of Allah *(AJ)*. They remind you of Sayyidina Muhammad (ﷺ). They remind us of our obligations and our realities, which Allah *(AJ)* wants to dress us.

Reality Fana (Annihilation) and Baqa (Resurrection/Ever-Living)

If you have a name within that reality, then Allah *(AJ)* grants you to go deeper. Now come into the oceans of non-existence, that even Imam 'Ali *(as)* said, "I have an annihilation within my annihilation." It means if you got that far, they taught you how to annihilate yourself. Then again there must be another annihilation within your  annihilation to enter the oceans of nothingness. You must have a name in that *fana*. And if Allah *(AJ)* grants that *fana* and grants you to be resurrected in His Divinely Presence, that is the 11th month.

To be nothing you came through Ramadan; to be '1' and '0', binary. They teach you to be nothing, be nothing, enter the ocean of *fana*, be nothing Allah *(AJ)* is everything! Then *baqa* is let us raise him in our Divinely Presence and turn him 'on'. At that time from being 'off' you will be 'on' and you will be reflection of this reality. That enters into the 12th month of the Hajj.

Who is Your Lord? 7 Names Were Meant to Govern You

That is the reality of the Hajj. That we are making seven *tawaf* for our seven Paradise realities, and we have a name in each of these Paradises. That our whole life is based on that *tawaf*, that it never ends. It is not a trip and a vacation that you take once, but a continuous one in our lives. A struggle to know ourselves, to know all of this lordship, that Allah *(AJ)* dressed upon the soul; "That is the lordship that I had intended for you."

These seven names and seven realities were meant to be the Lord over you, means that which governs you in life. Those names were

Secret Realities of Hajj

supposed to govern you; your Paradise reality was supposed to be governing you, and *dunya* came and deceived us and made Shaytan to be Lord over us. Anyone says "no" then say, "Okay you must be seeing, you must be able to walk on water." If we had the dress that Allah *(AJ)* intended for us, so many amazing realities. But what is lord over us are the desires and and the wants and the bad characteristics.

We pray Allah *(AJ)* dress us from the realities of *tawaf* and dress us from the realities of Hajj. Dress us from the Light and the love of Sayyidina Muhammad (ﷺ), from *Ashaab an-Nabi* (ﷺ), from *Ashaab an-Nabi* (ﷺ) and all *awliyaullah* from the Heavens and on Earth.

Subhana rabbika rabil 'izzati 'ama yasifoon, Wa salamun 'alal mursaleen wal hamdulillahi rabbil 'alameen. Bi hurmati Muhammadil Mustafa wa bi siratil suratil Fatiha.

THE SEVEN SPRINGS OF REALITY

Secrets of Safa wa al Marwah
Openings of the Zamzam

By Mawlana Shaykh Hisham Kabbani

Al-hal is the inner state of a person, which determines to what level he will be raised and how he experiences inspiration through his heart.

- In large part, *hal* is the result of his *amal*.
- *Al-feyd* is an external emanation or outpouring of heavenly light sent directly by Allah *(AJ)*, which descends on that person without his influence or interference. The two generate distinct feelings within the person.

Grandshaykh AbdAllah said these different characteristics come to people from seven different springs, each which flows from a unique source. The different states people experience are influenced by the specific types of angels that Allah *(AJ)* assigns to help them progress from one internal state to another.

The First Spring

The first level of heavenly springs from among the seven is conducted by angels specifically created and assigned by Allah *(AJ)* to inspire the actions of His servants.

- These angels send thoughts, inspirations and power, all of which change the person in a way that is outwardly apparent.
- These angels are essentially directing him through inspiration. He experiences expanded states of happiness and elation, or constricted states of distraction and unhappiness.
- At this level, he is either in a state of expansion or constriction.
- Depending on how his heart processes the inspiration that moves him to these different states, either he will laugh, cry, or be in a state of confusion. Also, how his heart processes these inspirations is determined by his *amal*.
- If he does something wrong he might cry or be repentant, if he does something good he might be happy or satisfied that Allah *(AJ)* is happy with him.
- If he is kind on every occasion, *mashaAllah*, making *dhikr*, happy, receiving Allah's *tajalli*, he will be in a state of ecstasy, smiling, or crying out of love of Allah *(AJ)* or from fearing Him.
- All these various feelings are inspired by these angels, and are known as *hal*: internal states experienced by Allah's *(AJ)* servants.

Everything on this earth is maintained and supervised by angels to whom Allah *(AJ)* assigned specific tasks and responsibilities.

The Second Spring

The second spring that reaches Allah's *(AJ)* servant is conducted by another type of angel which makes him aware of what he has achieved.

- In order to progress to a higher spiritual level, sometimes people find they are in a bad situation that they deeply regret, and suddenly that situation leads to what we call *faraj*, a positive opening for them in their lives, which brings them happiness.
- The type of people we become is based upon our good and bad *`amal*, upon the good and bad positions we've taken in life, and the good and bad influences we've had around us.
- This is the basis of the science of psychology (*`amal al-nafs*), which reveals the psychology and personality of a person. However, such study cannot determine one's spiritual rank.

The Third Spring

The third spring is different. On the Day of Promises, when all things were atoms in the Divine Presence, when Allah *(AJ)* created your essence, your secrets, your *dhat*.

- He also assigned you to the care of your *murshid*, who guides you through your internal states into the role you are destined to assume in this life, and in ways to improve yourself.
- The *murshid* knows what inspirations the angels bring to your heart, guides you to the best outcome, and removes your confusion.
- When the *feyd* descends on you, the *murshid* channels it in a way that will raise you to higher spiritual levels.
- Thus, for the benefit of the *murid*, the *murshid* balances *hal* and *feyd*, the internal states along with heavenly emanations.

Secret Realities of Hajj

- Although there are hundreds of *Murshid at-Tabarruk*, *Murshid at-Tazkiyyah*, and *Murshid at-Tasfiyya*,
- in every century there is only one *Murshid at-Tarbiyya*: the one who is carrying the *Flag of Irshad* (guidance) Mawlana Shaykh Hisham Al Kabbani.

- He is the source, the spring that flows from the heart of knowledge.
- He receives guidance directly from the Prophet (ﷺ) and disseminates it to all other *awliya*.
- While there are 124,000 different *awliya* at any given time, there is only one inheritor of Prophet (ﷺ).
- He has the ability and permission to raise the *awliya*, and they can raise all of us.
- When the *Murshid at-Tarbiyya* passes from this *dunya*, he passes on the inheritance he received from Prophet (ﷺ) to another *wali*.
- In this way, at any given time there is only one *Murshid at-Tarbiyya* in the world. Allah *(AJ)* gave the permission to Prophet (ﷺ) - and from Prophet (ﷺ) to that *murshid* - to have a connection with all the *awliya*, even those in *hayyat al-Barzakh*.

- To take benefit from the *awliya*, the *Murshid at-Tarbiyya* identifies what powers and specialties they each have, which he takes from them and passes to *Murshid at-Tabarruk*, *Murshid at-Tazkiyyah*, *Murshid at-Tasfiyya*, and to his followers.
- However, only those who reach the level of *murid* in Naqshbandi *tariqat*, who reach the highest level of guidance and who are seekers on that path can benefit from the *awliya* of *Barzakh*, and even then, only through the *murshid*.
- To truly communicate with and take benefit from souls in the grave one must have conquered his ego, and his sole aim must be the Divine Presence.
- These special people are under the guidance of the *Murshid at-Tazkiyya* and they have reached a subtle state of existence in this world.
- Average human beings cannot take benefit from the people of *Barzakh* because they do not have that connection, and are therefore unable to receive inspiration or guidance from *awliya* who have passed into the next world, who no longer use their physical powers.
- However, average people can benefit greatly from the living *awliya*, as they comprehend life through the physical realm. As such, living *awliya* are able to reach them on both physical and spiritual levels.
- When one seeks the way of Allah *(AJ)* in any of the forty-one *tariqats*, and did not reach the level of high-ranking *wali*, the order will come for him to complete his seclusion in the grave.
- The duration of that seclusion will be from forty days to five or seven years, and it is 70,000 times more difficult that the seclusion in this world.
- One who completed his seclusion in this world and who has attained the subtle state of existence here in *dunya*, will be higher in spiritual station than one who reached a subtle state of existence in the grave.

Secret Realities of Hajj

The third spring comes to us when we keep the orders of the *Murshid at-Tazkiyya*, following his guidance, following the footsteps of Sayyidina Muhammad (ﷺ), doing the specific daily *awrad* we are assigned, offering *dhikr-ullah* and all the prayers on time, observing all the *sunnah* of Prophet. When this outward conduct is achieved our hearts begin to move, like one who breathes quickly.

The heart palpitates and the *murid* "catches on fire".

The Fourth Spring

At this level, the fourth spring reaches him and he begins to receive heavenly blessings, because he received from the angels of the first and second springs, from the *Murshid at-Tazkiyya*, following the *awrad* and *sunnah*, resulting in Allah's *(AJ)* mercy descending on him.

Now his heart begins to palpitate, and the

The Fifth Spring

The fifth spring comes to him.

- Every Thursday and Monday, in the association of *awliya-ullah*, every *murshid* spiritually presents his followers and their *amal* to Prophet Muhammad (ﷺ).
- Those *murids* whose hearts are palpitating will be brought into the presence of Prophet (ﷺ), simply by the *murshid* saying, "*Ya Sayyidi*, this is my *murid* from your *ummah*. He is following your orders and seeking *Sirat al-Mustaqeem*, following in the footsteps of the *awliya*."
- Allah *(AJ)* said in Holy Qur`an: First they believe, then they disbelieve, then they fall completely.

- *Kufra* here does not refer to entering a state of *kufr*, but rather means to fall into sin. *Summa amanu* here means that he begins to perform more good *amal*, and afterwards follows the path of Shaytan, then falls completely.
- He is Muslim, but still falling into sin. At this point, *Murshid at-Tazkiyya* is deep in concentration on the hearts of his followers, preparing them and building them up in order that they not fall into mischief.
- That is why he presents them to the Prophet (ﷺ) every Thursday and Monday in the *majlis* of *awliya*, in which Prophet (ﷺ) examines what each *murshid* achieved with their *murids*.
- So when Prophet (ﷺ) observes the *murid* following his *sunnah*, observing the ways of *awliya-ullah*, he becomes very happy and accepts the *amal* of the *murid* and begins to direct his vision to that *murid*.
- From Prophet's happiness, the *feyd* - Allah's *(AJ)* satisfaction, blessings, divine Lights – begins to reach that *murid*.
- This is why Muslims say, *Unzur Alaina Ya Rusul-allah* "Oh Rasul-allah, look at us, give us one vision, one glance! We are under your *tajalli*, listen to our request, our *du`a*, for we are praising you, and we are drowning in difficulties which we beg you to remove."
- When Prophet (ﷺ) is happy with the *murid* of that shaykh, he will look at that person, raise him up, and Allah's *(AJ)* blessing comes on the *murid*.
- As he is raised up, the heart of that *murid* will begin to beat in complete ecstasy, turning, whirling in Allah's *(AJ)* love.

The Sixth Spring

Then Allah *(AJ)* inspires the *murid* to reach the sixth spring. At this level, when the *murid* begins to recite Holy Qur`an - Allah's *(AJ)* ancient words –

Secret Realities of Hajj

- Allah *(AJ)* will assign a *tajalli* for each letter, word and verse, which goes quietly to its target, the *murid's* heart, where it affects change.
- Without that *tajalli* there is no change.
- One can read the Holy Qur`an day and night, and interpret what they read according to their limited understanding, take wisdom from it, and even become enlightened.
- But one cannot have a vision unless that *tajalli* comes with the recitation, which reaches you when the Prophet (ﷺ) becomes happy with you, resulting in Allah *(AJ)* opening that *tajalli*.

After one enters these six different levels,

The Seventh Spring

Allah *(AJ)* allows them to reach the seventh spring,

- through which He opens the secret of the essence of their birth.

The Spring of Innocence

The Prophet (ﷺ) said:

"A child is born in innocence."

Prophet (ﷺ) also said if the pipe of the servant is still connected with his origin, with his heavenly source.

- Allah *(AJ)* opens to him the "Spring of Innocence", *fitrat al-Islam*, the seventh spring.
- That channel is like a plumbing pipe, running water directly from the original source all the way to the tap, connecting the *murid* with *alam al-arwah*.
- That pipe is always there.
- Our unique reality comes from our essence *(dhat)*, the atom Allah *(AJ)* created on the Day of Promises, the day of *alastu bi rabbikum kalu bala*, when Allah *(AJ)* asked each of us, "Am I not your Lord and you are My servant?" and we answered,
- "Yes!" From that day, *ibadullah*, Allah's *(AJ)* servants, have been in a state of worship until their spirits reached the womb of their mothers.
- From that day each soul has remained in a continuous state of worship, without cessation.
- At that heavenly event, Allah *(AJ)* assigned obligations to each soul, and angels who assist them in their worship.
- In that state of servitude, each soul is engaged in pure worship of their Lord, with no *shirk*.
- Allah *(AJ)* may choose to raise anyone and bestow His *feyd* upon them.
- In each moment, Allah *(AJ)* dresses His servants in *anwar al-nabi* that first comes to Prophet (ﷺ), and from Prophet (ﷺ) to *anbiya* and *awliya*, and from *awliya* to everyone else.

- Just as Sayyidina Adam *(as)* was dressed by Allah *(AJ)* in Paradise, in every moment Allah *(AJ)* dresses His servant who is in His Divine Presence with 70,000 different *tajalli*.
- Paradise is always a living existence, where pain and harm do not exist.
- All Allah's *(AJ)* servants, every soul, lived in Paradise before they were born into this world.
- There Allah *(AJ)* crowns everyone with divine ecstasy, and with *Sifat al-Jamal*.
- They are completely pure in that ecstasy, and from within that state they desire the utmost love and beauty, from that attribute of *Sifat al-Jamal lillahi ta'ala*.
- Anyone born in *dunya* was first born in Paradise. When the time comes, he appears in dunya through his mother's womb.
- This is why every child cries at birth, from the pain and shock of separation from holy presence. At the time of birth into this world, every baby makes du`a, pleading with Allah *(AJ)* to allow them to return to that holy presence.
- Some babies die immediately after birth, because Allah *(AJ)* accepts their *du`a* and takes them back!

No one came into *dunya* laughing or smiling; they cry! Only Prophet (ﷺ) didn't cry when he came to *dunya*; he immediately recited *ummati ummati*, "My nation, My nation," and went into *sajdah*, asking Allah *(AJ)* to protect his *ummah*.

Sayyidina Isa *(as)* didn't cry when he came to *dunya*; he said, *inni abdullah*!

Babies cry when they are born, because they fear now they will be tempted to sin and will not know what to do. Prophet (ﷺ) said that when a child is born, either his parents make him a Jew, a Christian or a Zoroastrian, while in fact the child is already Muslim, because that pre-existing heavenly *`ilm* and worship cannot be darkened. So if that child comes to *dunya* and begins to deviate from what he was previously taught in Paradise, he becomes veiled from heavenly powers. If his parents are not observing states of ritual purity and prayer, if they expose him to different bad characters, he will be veiled to the Divine reality.

At the time of birth he can still see, he still has that vivid link to Paradise, but when he is veiled that vision is completely veiled. However, in His Mercy, Allah *(AJ)* preserves all the blessing and light associated with that baby's worship in Paradise! So when he reaches the age of obligation (adulthood), Allah *(AJ)* restores to him the benefit of all his worship that he performed in his spiritual life in the Divine Presence.

That person might sin and repent, sin again and repent again, but he will still be credited with that previous worship.

That's why when someone is given back to their heart, they are happy. Sometimes you feel so happy and you don't know why. There is no reason or explanation, just happiness. You feel light, with no troubles. Allah *(AJ)* knows you are a sincere servant, and He opens more for you from that heavenly presence, if fills your heart, and you find yourself in a state of contentment. About this Allah *(AJ)* said, *ala bi dhikr-ullahi tatmainnul qulub*, "In Allah's remembrance hearts find satisfaction, relaxation!"

The human body is a physical form subject to physical laws. It is dense and gravity pulls in down, holding it to the earth. If we use the example of a metal cylinder filled with helium gas, the cylinder is heavy. However, by changing the density of the helium, it can fill a balloon that will ascend up into the atmosphere. When Allah *(AJ)* restores all your previous *dhikr*, it fills you like a helium balloon, and you feel light. When your previous prayers and *dhikr* enter the prison of your physical body and Allah *(AJ)* releases that holy energy, it balances you between the two worlds and makes you happy.

By Allah's *(AJ)* order to Prophet (ﷺ), and from Prophet (ﷺ) to *awliya-ullah* who are responsible for your *Murshid at-Tarbiyya*, that energy is released. It raises you up and changes your system, completely freeing you from all kinds of depression, and you relax. You are reconnected with your reality that previously, because of yourself and the darkness of this *dunya*, you were unable to see, and you will begin to see things that others cannot see.

Following the way of Sayyidina Jalaluddin Rumi [q], the Mevlavi *tariqat* practices a form of whirling that thrusts them into that pure state of ecstasy, when Allah *(AJ)* releases that holy power to Prophet (ﷺ), and Prophet (ﷺ) releases it to *awliya-ullah*. This is what Sayyidina Jalaluddin Rumi experienced. When you go up, you don't go straight - you turn!

When the helicopter ascends its propeller spins, creating the power that thrusts it up off the ground. He was not dancing; he was spinning to that energy taking him upward.

- The reality of spinning is like electrons spinning around the nucleus of the atom. When Allah *(AJ)* released that energy, Jalaluddin Rumi was spinning around his essence, his reality.
- It connected him directly to his reality in the Divine Presence (from the Day of Promises), and he was surprised by what Allah *(AJ)* granted him.
- When Muslims perform Hajj, we perform *tawaf* in the same way that electrons circumambulate the nucleus, in a counter-clockwise direction.
- This makes us spin, in order to raise us to heavens.
- There are higher, spiritual ranks of *tawaf* above every person. *Awliya-ullah* make *tawaf* (spiritually) immediately above the people, and angels make *tawaf* above the *awliya-ullah*, ascending all the way up to *Baytul Ma'mur*, up to the Divine Throne.

- Everything must spin around its reality.
- The reality of the atom is located in the nucleus.
- The electron, its energy, is running after its essence.
- We have to spin around our essence.
- If we can expose our essence and our energy, and make our energy spin around our essence, at that time we can raise our body — like a condensed gas released in a balloon. In this state we are able to fly.

This is the seventh power of knowledge: the "spring of innocence" of Islam,

- which Allah *(AJ)* has given to every person.
- In addition, Allah *(AJ)* rewards believers with all the benefit that unbelievers achieved through their spiritual light from the Day of Promises, to the day of coming to *dunya*.
- That's why believers are raised higher so quickly. For example, if we were to say, "Here are one hundred gold coins to be divided among anyone who needs them." If one hundred people needed the coins, each person would get one coin.
- If ten people needed the coins, each would get ten, and so on.

Anyone who believes in and follows Allah *(AJ)* and His Prophet (ﷺ), and follows the Divine message and the Way *(tariqat)* of their *shaykh*, especially the *Murshid at-Tarbiyya*, will inherit the huge blessings which Allah *(AJ)* gave everyone on the Day of Promises, and the benefit of every unbeliever's worship from that Day until they came to *dunya*.

Further, in these times when corruption is so widespread, believers get even more benefit. Prophet (ﷺ) said, *min ahiya sunnati inda fasadi ummati falahu ajrun sab'eena shaheed aw miya shaheed,* "When everyone leaves my *sunnah*, when there will be corruption throughout my nation,

- Allah *(AJ)* will give the one who revives one *sunnah* the reward of seventy martyrs or one hundred martyrs." This applies to praying *sunnah rak`ats* of prayer,
- wearing a ring,
- keeping a beard,
- using *miswak*, and in fact any *sunnah* of the Prophet (ﷺ).
- As those people did not keep their promise to Allah *(AJ)* to believe in and worship Him alone, Allah *(AJ)* has chosen to give the benefit of their past worship to those who kept their promise.
- That is why the *ajrhas* increased in these last days.
- So this is a summary of the seventh spring, which can be reached through spinning around your essence.
- When the feyd reaches you, you will experience every moment in a state of continuous ecstasy that will not cease until the day you die.
- You will reach the level about which Allah *(AJ)* spoke, *mutu kabla anta mu'tu*, "Die (overcome your ego) before you die."
- The Prophet (ﷺ) said, "If you want to see anyone who died before he died, look at Abu Bakr as-Siddiq *(ra)*."
- It means Sayyidina Abu Bakr *(ra)* was able control his ego and the four enemies.
- So when one follows in the footsteps of Sayyidina Abu Bakr as-Siddiq *(ra)*, it leads to the Way of Sayyidina Muhammad (ﷺ), which leads to that state of ecstasy, where one spins around their essence in a very high velocity that causes them to rise up! When they rise, there is nothing to stop them from rising higher.
- Like a tornado: it continues to spin until it cannot be seen anymore, because it lifted up from earth.
- In this higher state one creates an ideal environment that has no friction, no darkness, no bad desires, no sins, and nodunya.

- In that environment one proceeds toward the Heavenly Presence that Allah *(AJ)* wants them to reach. This is why *awliya-ullah* do not chase *dunya*, as it has no value for them.
- They are preoccupied with that heavenly pleasure, that state of continuous ecstasy that increases each moment, which in their world diminishes *dunya* to nothing.

Many condemn the dervishes who sit in the corner reciting *dhikr-ullah*, because they don't know what kind of happiness these dervishes are experiencing! If a minute ray of light is opened from the Divine light falling on those dervishes, it will drown everyone in this *dunya* with that ecstasy.

So why would those dervishes want to leave that ecstasy for *dunya*? The goal of every *mu'min* and Muslim is to do good `amal* so when he faces his Lord on Judgment Day, Allah *(AJ)* is happy with him.

Those dervishes have already reached that level! May Allah forgive us, and help us understand the Way of *awliya-ullah*.

Don't be a prisoner to your inner self, to your ego and the four enemies - *nafs, dunya, hawa, Shaytan* – be a free person! Otherwise you will be a loser on the Day of Judgment.

Don't ask to be an orphan! All their lives orphans experience *nar al-hasra*, the fire that burns from within, caused by the loss of something so precious.

- Don't lose your first father, your *murshid*!
- Don't be an orphan without a *murshid*!
- Find your guide! Find *Murshid at-Tarbiyya*, who can raise you up.
- Don't make the mistake of thinking you don't need anyone, that you can proceed directly without a guide.

Secret Realities of Hajj

- Keep the spiritual father who guides you to Allah *(AJ)*. *Murshid at-Tarbiyya* will make you happy in this life and in the Hereafter, pulling you to your divine station through his guidance.
- If you follow his guidance, you will attract *feyd al-ilahi*, the emanations of Allah's *(AJ)* blessings. *Wa min Allah at-Tawfiq*. And success is with Allah *(AJ)*.

Subhana rabbika rabil 'izzati 'ama yasifoon, Wa salamun 'alal mursaleen wal hamdulillahi rabbil 'alameen. Bi hurmati Muhammadil Mustafa wa bi siratil suratil Fatiha.

Appendix 1

Welcoming the Holy Month of Dhul Hijjah and 'Arafah

On the day before the first day of Dhul Hijjah (30th day of Dhul Qi'dah – 11th Lunar month), it is recommended to do the following practices;

After Salatul 'Asr (before sunset) prayer

1. Perform the Major ritual Purification (Ghusul/Shower)
2. Dress in the best clothes
3. Make Wudu (ablution)
4. Pray 2 *raka'at Salatul Tahyatul Wudu* (Pray two-cycle regular prayer)
5. Make Niyyat (Intention) by reciting:

نَوَيْتُ الْاَرْبَعِينْ، نَوَيْتُ الْاَعْتِكَافْ، نَوَيْتُ الْخَلْوَة، نَوَيْتُ الْعِزْلَة، نَوَيْتُ الرِّيَاضَة، نَوَيْتُ السُّلُوكَ وَالصِّيَامْ لِلّٰهِ تَعَالَى اَلْعَظِيمْ فِيْ هَذَا الْمَسْجِدْ
(الْجَامِعْ فِيْ هَذَا)

Nawaytul Arba'een, Nawaytul 'itikaf, Nawaytul Khalwah
Nawaytul 'Uzlah, Nawaytur Riyada, Nawaytus Sulook wa Siyam,
Lillahi Ta`ala l 'Azhim fee hadhal masjid* (or *fee hadhal jami`)

"I intend the forty (days of seclusion), I intend seclusion in the mosque, I intend seclusion, I intend isolation, I intend discipline (of the ego), I intend to travel in God's Path, I intend to fast, for the sake of God in this mosque."

To have the intention that Allah *(AJ)* makes me to meet spiritually with Rasulullah (ﷺ), Imam al Mahdi *(as)* and Mawlana Shaykh.

Appendix 2

Fasting in the First Ten Days of Dhul Hijjah

The first ten days of Dhul Hijjah is very holy and people try to fast as many days as they can from those ten days. It is *mustahabb* (highly recommended) for those who are not pilgrims to fast on the day of 'Arafah.

It is Recommended to fast:

- 9th of Dhul Hijjah – Yawmmul 'Arafah – (Day of 'Arafat)

Prophet Muhammad (ﷺ) said:
"Fasting the day of 'Arafat expiates the sins of two years: a past one and a coming one…" [Muslim (no. 1162)]

Imam Ghazali said in *'Ihya' 'Ulum al-Din'*:
"Fasting is definitely desirable in certain meritorious days, some of them being found in every year, others in every month, and others in every week. Those that are found in every year after the days of Ramadan are:

- The Day of *'Arafah* [9th of *Dhul Hijjah*]
- The Day of *'Ashura* [10th of *Muharram*]
- The first Ten Days of *Dhul Hijjah*
- The first ten days of *Muharram*

And all the sacred months are preferred for fasting… and they are:
- *Dhul Qi'dah*
- *Dhul Hijjah*
- *Muharram* and
- *Rajab."*

Appendix 3

Significance of the First Ten Days and Nights of Dhul Hijjah

'Abd Allah ibn Mas'ud said: The Prophet (ﷺ) said:

"There are no days in the year in which deeds are more meritorious than in the Ten Days [i.e. the first ten days of Dhul Hijjah]." Someone asked: "Not even Jihad in the path of Allah?" He replied: "Not even Jihad in the path of Allah." Haythami said: "Tabarani narrated it in *al Mu'jam al-kabir* and the narrators in its chain of transmission are all those of sound (*sahih*) narrations.

The nights are included in the mention of the days. Allah *(AJ)* swore an oath by them when He said: "*By the Dawn! By Ten Nights!*" (89:1-2) and the authors of *Tafsir al-Jalalayn* said: "They are the first ten nights of Dhul Hijjah."

وَالْفَجْرِ (١) وَلَيَالٍ عَشْرٍ ٢

68:1-2 – "Wal Fajr. Wa layalin 'ashr." (Surah al Fajr)

"By the Dawn. And [by] ten nights." (Holy Quran 68:1-2)

Appendix 4

Prayer and Sacrifice in `Eid Ul Adha (Feast of Sacrifice)

لَبَّيْكَ اللَّهُمَّ لَبَّيْكَ، لَبَّيْكَ لاَ شَرِيكَ لَكَ لَبَّيْكَ، إِنَّ الْحَمْدَ، وَالنِّعْمَةَ، لَكَ وَالْمُلْكَ، لاَ شَرِيكَ لَكَ

Labbayk Allahumma Labbayk, Labbayka la sharika laka Labbayk, Innal Hamda, wan Ni'mata laka wal Mulk, La sharika lak.

"Here I am O Allah (Allahumma), Here I am. You have no partner, here I am. Verily all praise and blessings, and all sovereignty/Kingdom are Yours, You have no partner."

- It is recommended not to eat anything on the day of `Eid al-Adha* until one perform the Prayer.
- It is recommended to perform *ghusl* (major ablution) before the prayer, any time after *Fajr* even if one does not attend the prayer.
- It is recommended for men to dress their best and wear perfume.

- It is *Sunnah* to come to the mosque early and on foot, and to return home by a different route.

It is preferable for a *`Eid* Congregation to pray outdoors. The *`Eid* prayer is a *Sunnah mu'akkada* or confirmed *Sunnah* and is recommended to be prayed in congregation. It is *wajib* (obligatory) in the Hanafi *madhhab* and therefore required of every person who is required to perform *Jum'ah*, i.e. healthy male residents of the region in which it is performed.

It is a *Sunnah mu'akkada* and, in the Hanafi *madhhab*, a *wajib*, for every adult Muslim man and woman to sacrifice at least one *shat* — a sheep or a goat — for *`Eid al Adha*. This may be done any time after the prayer on the first day of *`Eid* until sunset on the last of the two days following the first day. One may have someone else perform the sacrifice on his behalf, whether in his presence or in absence.

Appendix 5

Complete the Sunnah of Qurban (Sacrifice)

From The Naqshbandi Center of Vancouver and Mawlana Shaykh As-Sayed Nurjan Mirahmadi

Getting Ready for the Holy month of Pilgrimage (Hajj). The Days of Qurban, sacrifice, for the sake of Allah *(AJ)* are approaching with Dhul Hijjah. We remind everyone that the *udhiya* is a *Sunnah Mu'akkadah* (confirmed action of the Prophet ﷺ) in the *madhhabs* of Imam Malik, Ahmad bin Hanbal and Imam Shafi`ee and it is *wajib* (required) in the *madhhab* of Imam Abu Hanifah.

This is an excellent time to give in the Way of Allah *(AJ)* and to receive the *tajalli's* of this holy month. If you are not already doing so, please consider signing-up for monthly support through PayPal. Giving monthly support allows us the opportunity to become a shareholder in these blessings, so that our families can be dressed by them, and is highly recommended. All donations are tax deductible at the end of the year, inshallah.

وَسَيُجَنَّبُهَا الْأَتْقَى (١٧) الَّذِي يُؤْتِي مَالَهُ يَتَزَكَّىٰ (١٨)

92:17-18 – *"Wa sayujannabuha al atqa. Al ladhi yutee maalahu, yatazakka." (Surah al Layl)*

"But the righteous one [who is conscious of Allah] will avoid it [hell fire]. *Those who spend their wealth to Purify himself/ increase in self-purification." (Holy Quran, The Night)*

All proceeds go towards supporting the Center and its programs. Therefore it is also considered money spent in the Way of Allah *(AJ)*. Every donation we give, takes away many difficulties from our lives and surrounds us and our loved ones with blessings. If you would like to give a donation you may do so online or give personally to Mawlana Shaykh Nurjan, inshallah. May Allah *(AJ)* reward everyone here and Hereafter for their generosity and their commitment to supporting the true message of Islam in these difficult times!

To support and complete the Sunnah of Qurban (Sacrifice) of *Eid ul Adha*, please contact the **Naqshbandi Nazimiya of Vancouver** as early as you can.

www.ingramcontent.com/pod-product-compliance
Lightning Source LLC
Chambersburg PA
CBHW070631300426
44113CB00010B/1729